DON'T LET GO OF THE ROPE!

HEARTWARMING STORIES OF HOPE AND ENCOURAGEMENT

Don't Let Go of the Rope!

We Need Each Other

Heartwarming Stories of Hope and Encouragement

Walter Albritton

Other Books By Walter Albritton

If You Want to Walk on Water, You've Got to Get Out of Your Boat

Life is Short So Laugh Often, Live Fully, and Love Deeply

*Do the Best You Can With What You've Got,
Where You Are, While There's Time*

Just Get Over It And Move On!

You Simply Can't Trust a Talking Bird

*Lord, Please Deliver Me, I Beg You,
From Another Live Manger Scene*

An Exciting Saturday Night Ride in An Ambulance

Available from Christian bookstores
or from
www.walteralbritton.org

Dedicated To

Tony Barkley

Jere Beasley

Richard Brown

Ted Cheek

Eddie Davis

Nathan Hamilton

Charles Henson

John Howard

Jim Hutchens

Roy Jordan

Greg Lotz

John Nichols

Robert Powell

Cecil Spear

Jack Swarthout

Ron Wilkinson

Jack Yancey

*These men have been dear friends and companions
on our journey with Christ but more than that,
they are authentic disciples of Jesus Christ
who have rope burns on their hands.*

Introduction

I love a good story. Stories help us understand the meaning of life. Most sermons miss their mark unless the preacher can illustrate the truth with a few good stories. So relentlessly I have looked for stories that could bring life to my preaching and writing.

God loves stories too. The Bible is filled with wonderful stories of people struggling with the same issues of life that we all wrestle with. Wise and effective preachers and teachers use biblical stories to make the Gospel come alive to their listeners.

Our friends have wonderful stories to tell – if we take the time to listen. Their stories can enrich our lives and encourage us in our own journey. Sooner or later we learn that we cannot make the journey alone; we need each other. At one time or another each of us is a "basket case" and needs friends who will hold the rope to keep us from falling. There have been many times when my life was in the hands of good friends who were holding the rope to keep me from falling. I am so thankful they loved me enough not to let go of the rope.

Once we experience the help of others, we will find times when we are strong enough to hold the rope for a friend in the basket. To assist someone else gives meaning and dignity to our own lives. Such occasions teach us the true meaning of love. It illustrates what Jesus meant when he said, "You are brothers."

My hope is that in these pages you will find a few stories that will inspire you to be thankful for those who rescue you in your hour of need, and motivate you to hold the rope when a brother or sister needs your help.

At the end of life you should have rope burns on your hands. Surely this is what Jesus had in mind when he commanded us to "Love each other as I have loved you."

Walter Albritton, sjc
Servant of Jesus Christ

The Cabin
Wetumpka, Alabama
July, 2010

Contents

Don't let go of the rope

The man the Church calls "Saint Paul" was brilliant. And his exceptional mind was not wasted. He studied the Hebrew Old Testament at the feet of the famous teacher Gamaliel to become, in his own words, "a Pharisee of the Pharisees." Until he met Jesus Paul, who was known then as Saul of Tarsus, was very proud of his heritage and his credentials.

Paul's meeting with Jesus occurred on the Damascus Road and it was a humbling experience. Determined to rid the world of those who called themselves followers of Jesus, Paul was on his way to Damascus to capture Christians and bring them bound to Jerusalem. On the outskirts of the town Paul was stunned by a bright light "from heaven." Falling to the ground he heard the voice calling his name. The one speaking was Jesus who had been recently crucified.

Jesus explained to Paul that by persecuting Christians, he was persecuting him. Saint Luke, who describes this encounter in the Acts of the Apostles, says that Paul, "trembling and astonished," asked Jesus, "What do you want me to do?" Jesus told Paul to go into the city where he would receive his instructions.

Paul stood up but he had to have help to go into Damascus; the bright light had blinded him. Blind and bewildered, the once proud champion of Judaism was led by the hand into Damascus. There a disciple named Ananias prayed for him and as he did Paul's eyesight was restored and he was "filled with the Holy Spirit." Paul immediately embraced the Christian faith and was baptized. Thus began Paul's new mission – to proclaim the Gospel to the Gentiles.

The Damascus fellowship was fertile ground for Paul. He not only regained his sight; he grasped a totally new perspective on the growing Christian movement. Committed to Christ, Paul was carefully nurtured in the faith by the small band of believers in Damascus. Soon he began preaching in the synagogues that the Christ was the Son of God.

The Jews were confounded; the gifted Pharisee they had once trusted was suddenly preaching Christ in such a powerful way that "all who heard him were amazed." The Jews became so angry that they decided to kill Paul. Earlier Paul had been humbled by his unique encounter with Jesus. Now he was about to be humiliated. I will let Saint Luke explain how:

"Now after many days were past, the Jews plotted to kill him. But their plot became known to Saul. And they watched the gates day and night, to kill him. Then the disciples took him by night and let him down through the wall in a large basket" (Acts of the Apostles 9:23-25).

The proud scholar and former persecutor of Christians had become a basket case! We can imagine how humiliated Paul felt. He knows the Jews plan to kill him. He fears for his life. So he turns to his friends for help. They devise a plan of escape; they will put Paul in a large basket and in the dead of night lower it with ropes over the wall.

Put yourself in Paul's predicament. You would want to take a good look at the ropes; are they strong enough to hold the basket securely? Who is going to tie the knots? And of course, who is going to hold the rope and make sure Paul does not fall to his death? You would want to make sure some strong men were holding the rope, and not some scrawny little weaklings!

Think about it: for a moment in time the greatest evangelist in history, the man who wrote a great portion of the New Testament, was cowering in a basket, fearful for his life! His future, and the future of Christianity, was dependent upon a few nameless disciples who were holding the rope that held that basket. The great Apostle Paul – a basket case!

Paul's embarrassment surely must have raised questions in his mind. Is this what it will mean to follow Christ? Is the One who conquered death and hell on the cross unable to protect me from my enemies? Is God going to allow me to be crucified in the same way his own Son was put to death?

There are helpful lessons in this story for those who are followers of the Way today. Paul's basket is an appropriate symbol of the meaning of Christian discipleship. In our journey with Christ there will be occasions when each of us is a basket case needing the help of Christian friends. At other times each of us will be called upon to hold the rope for others.

Along the way the harsh realities of life can overwhelm us. Discouraged and afraid, we may find that we are unable to cope or stand in our own strength. We need the help of others. In such times our friends in the fellowship come to our aid; they hold the rope for us until the crisis is past.

This unmistakable lesson is clear: if you belong to Christ, you belong also to the others who belong to Christ, and you will often have rope burns on your hands! If you never have rope burns, as a result of holding the rope for others, then you do not truly belong to that fellowship known as His Body.

I know what it feels like to be a basket case, to be humiliated by circumstances beyond my control. And I also know the unspeakable joy that was mine when some of my friends held the rope for me until I recovered. It often stirs my soul to realize that some of my dearest friends have rope burns on their hands because of me. They were there when I needed strong hands to hold the rope. The awareness of their love prompts me to be available when someone in trouble needs me.

Genuine discipleship is a cooperative venture. When God helps us, he usually helps us through the fellowship of believers. We need each other, and we help each other. That is the nature of the Church. That is the way authentic love is expressed.

If you think this is merely "preacher talk," think again. In his book, **The Winners Manual for the Game of Life** (Tyndale House Publishers, 2008), Ohio State Head Football Coach Jim Tressel has an entire chapter on love. Tressel insists that love and discipline are necessary for a team to reach its full potential. This is how he puts it:

"True winners in the game of life will not look merely at goals and achievements. True winners who are part of a winning team will care more about the people beside them in the trenches than they will about the trophy at the end of the journey. True winners will have compassion for their teammates and desire the good of others as well as their own."

I am certain that if we were to examine Coach Tressel's hands, we would find rope burns on them! More than once he has been in the trenches, holding the rope for his players and coaches.

The humiliation of basket times in our lives can become the doorway to great service for God. It was so with Saint Paul. It was so with King David. It was so for the Apostle Peter. It has been so with many of my Christian friends. And it has been so with me.

Take a good look at your hands. If you do not find some fresh rope burns on your hands, perhaps it is not too late to offer your help to some hurting friend. Surely the cry of your heart is the same as my own: When I am in the basket, please don't let go of the rope! +

X

²²**Then came the Feast of Dedication at Jerusalem.** It was winter, ²³and Jesus was in the temple area walking in Solomon's Colonnade. ²⁴The Jews gathered around him, saying, "How long will you keep us in suspense? If you are the Christ, tell us plainly."

²⁵Jesus answered, "I did tell you, but you do not believe. The miracles I do in my Father's name speak for me, ²⁶but you do not believe because you are not my sheep. ²⁷My sheep listen to my voice; I know them, and they follow me. ²⁸I give them eternal life, and they shall never perish; no one can snatch them out of my hand. ²⁹My Father, who has given them to me, is greater than all; no one can snatch them out of my Father's hand. ³⁰I and the Father are one." John 10:22-30

We are his sheep. Though some of us spend many years feeding his sheep, our basic identity is not that of sheep feeders. We are sheep, the Lord's sheep. In the midst of the world's noises, we heard His voice and we began following him. Now, in the sunset years of our lives, when our friends are dying and we realize that we too will die soon, we very much need hope for the future.

Thankfully we have that hope. It is a hope not born of wishful thinking but a hope grounded in the promises of our Shepherd, who is the Word of God. Our Shepherd says of us, "I give them eternal life, and they shall never perish; no one can snatch them out of my hand. My Father, who has given them to me, is greater than all; no one can snatch them out of my Father's hand. I am the Father are one."

Jesus said it and I believe it. I have surrendered my life to the strong grip of my Lord Jesus and no one can snatch me out of his strong hand. Years ago I quit boasting that I had him; instead I began to rejoice that He has me. When fear creeps into my heart, it helps me to remember that I am held by His strong hand. Remembering helps us. Remember the words of Luke 22:19 – "And he took bread, gave thanks and broke it, and gave it to them, saying, "This is my body given for you; do this in remembrance of me."

Remembering is sobering. We know that one day soon our names will be among those read by those who gather for a memorial service. There are two significant ways that remembering helps us:

First, remembering reminds us what really matters. Affluence can blind us to the spiritual world. Materialism and pleasure can become too important to us. But death wakes us up like a slap in the face. Then we remember that our stuff is nothing compared to the possession of a compassionate heart.

Doctor Luke never tells us what stuff Jesus owned; he tells us that he had compassion on people – like the widow of Nain whose son had died. Jesus knew how devastated the woman was. She was destitute, having lost her husband and her son. She could not own land; she would be dependant upon her relatives and friends for food. So Jesus had compassion on her and raised her son back to life. At least three times we see Jesus having compassion on people, especially women, who had lost loved ones. He raised to life Jairus' daughter. And when he saw the grief of Mary and Martha for their brother Lazarus, Jesus raised him from the dead.

We are wise to pray for a compassionate heart more than the things of this world. Compassion is a characteristic of a truly mature human being. Compassion makes a difference anywhere, anytime. There are beautiful moments in my life when I was blessed by the compassion of others – like hearing Tom Chappell, our pastor, walking on crutches up the steps to visit our son David when he was dying of leukemia. Like the time my dear friend Ben Johnson showed up in the hospital to comfort me and my wife when our son Steve was facing critical surgery. Compassion really matters. Remembering that helps me.

Second, remembering reminds us of our own mortality. We too are going to die. By embracing that reality I can review my priorities and make whatever adjustments are needed to put first things first. So we are blessed to have the gift of memory. We remember what matters. We remember our own mortality. We remember the beauty of compassion. We remember that we are not leaves tossing in the winds of a storm; we are sheep held in the strong hand of the One who has given us the gift of eternal life.

Many years ago I chose Isaiah 41:10 as my most precious verse in the Old Testament. You remember the words: "Fear thou not; for I am with thee: be not dismayed; for I am thy God: I will strengthen thee; yea, I will help thee; yea, I will uphold thee with the right hand of my righteousness." Those are powerful words. Remembering them helps me – especially remembering that I am held by the Father's right hand.

In seminary one of my professors sharply criticized me for making God, in his words, too anthropomorphic. At first I was embarrassed. Then, because of the professor's criticism, I began to notice how anthropomorphic the Bible is about God. So often I read about the hand of God. The risen Christ, for example, is seated at the right hand of God. Peter says, "Humble yourselves, therefore, under God's mighty hand, that he may lift you up" (1 Peter 5:6). Finally I decided that my professor had complimented me with his criticism.

In Demopolis, Alabama, I got to know the family of Vern Humble. June and Vern have a daughter, April, who has never walked because of Spina bifida. April is past 50 now and she is a woman of faith, one of the Lord's special sheep. One day I got an email from her. She had read that Isaiah 41:10 was my favorite Old Testament verse. She said, "My favorite is Isaiah 41:13." I looked it up:

"For I the LORD thy God will hold thy right hand, saying unto thee, Fear not; I will help thee."

My verse 10 speaks of God's right hand. April's verse 13 told her that God will hold her by her right hand! I could see why April loved the verse.

April's message reminded me of the song I decided spontaneously to sing at my sister Laurida's funeral – "Precious Lord, take my hand." I nearly choked trying to sing the song and promised myself never to attempt singing again at a family member's funeral. You remember the song:

Precious Lord, take my hand
Lead me on, let me stand
I'm tired, I'm weak, I'm worn
Through the storm, through the night
Lead me on to the light
Take my hand precious Lord, lead me home

When my way grows drear precious Lord linger near
When my light is almost gone
Hear my cry, hear my call
Hold my hand lest I fall
Take my hand precious Lord, lead me home

When the darkness appears and the night draws near
And the day is past and gone
At the river I stand
Guide my feet, hold my hand
Take my hand precious Lord, lead me home

Precious Lord, take my hand
Lead me on, let me stand
I'm tired, I'm weak, I'm worn
Through the storm, through the night
Lead me on to the light
Take my hand precious Lord, lead me home

I know this: in the last hour of my life I could think of no better request than to say, "Precious Lord, ever since you accepted me as one of your sheep, you have held me in your strong hand. Now, precious Lord, take my hand and lead me home." And we need not be hesitant in asking God for his hand.

God reaches out his hand to us in many of our great songs of faith. One of my favorites is "How Firm a Foundation." After Andrew Jackson left the presidency he retired to his famous home, The Hermitage, outside Nashville, Tennessee. On his deathbed he asked the pastor visiting him to sing his favorite hymn, "How Firm a Foundation." The pastor invited others standing around Jackson's bed to sing the song with him and they sang it as the former president lay dying. Imagine how that must have blessed Andrew Jackson!

As you know it is a great hymn about the Bible and its promises. Verse one promises that God will provide a foundation for our faith in His excellent word:

"How firm a foundation, ye saints of the Lord, is laid for your faith in his excellent word! What more can he say than to you he has said, to you who for refuge to Jesus have fled?" Verse two promises that God will be with us, strengthen us, and help us:

"Fear not, I am with thee, O be not dismayed; For I am thy God, and will still give thee aid. I'll strengthen thee, help thee, and cause thee to stand, Upheld by my gracious, omnipotent hand."

Read

There once again the precious words of Isaiah 41 bless us:

I believe verses 10:00 to verse 13 — which is truth

¹⁰ So do not fear, for I am with you;
do not be dismayed, for I am your God.
I will strengthen you and help you;
I will uphold you with my righteous right hand.
¹³ For I am the LORD, your God, who takes hold of your right hand
and says to you, do not fear; I will help you.

My dear brothers and sisters, we need not fear death. Our Great Shepherd has conquered death and hell. Until He calls us home we can remember who we are and let Him give us peace about dying. We are his sheep. He has given us the gift of eternal life. And no one, absolutely no one, can snatch us out of his grasp. We can go to sleep at night with the calm assurance that we are Held by His Strong Hand. Amen and Amen! +

18

Touching the clay of young lives

In the category of "the unexpected," this week I received by email a picture of a fig tree. That is a "first" in my life. The sender was my friend Ed Williams. The healthy tree thrives "like crazy" in his backyard on Cedar Brook Drive in Auburn.

Ed is one of the reasons Auburn University is such a great school. Ed touches lives. He helps young people find their way. That is what he lives for. Ed serves as a professor in the Department of Communication and Journalism , but he does more than teach; he helps his students find a purpose for living.

Since 1985 Ed has been the beloved and effective faculty adviser for The Auburn Plainsman, the student newspaper recognized nationally for its excellence. Among other major college newspapers, only The Daily Texan (University of Texas) has received more Pacemaker Awards than The Plainsman. The Pacemaker Award is the equivalent of the Pulitzer Prize.

Like the legendary James Foy, Ed makes Auburn people thankful for the University of Alabama. He earned his bachelor's and master's degrees at the Capstone.

Ed's personal home page on the Internet alerts one quickly to the professor's easy going nature. The picture of a dog driving a car removes any likelihood that Ed is overly impressed with himself. In fact he says, "The most important thing I have learned over the years is the difference between taking one's work seriously and taking one's self seriously. The first is imperative, and the second disastrous."

Recently I heard a man say that his goal in life is to make a positive difference in the people whose lives he touches. He gave me a phrase I want to remember: "I try to touch the clay of other peoples' lives in a wonderful way." That, I think, is what Ed is doing at Auburn every day.

Perhaps you are wondering why Ed sent me a picture of the fig tree in his backyard. The reason says a lot about Ed. He remembered an article I wrote some months back about the fig tree in my backyard. He knew I would be blessed to know that he had recalled something I had written!

You can count on it – a smile broke across my face a mile wide and it stayed long enough to brighten my whole day! Every writer knows how difficult it is to compose something people will remember for three hours. I would probably faint if someone told me they remembered a comment I made in a sermon preached a year ago.

Yet Ed remembered my story about a fig tree. I had made the point that a jar of figs might save a man's marriage. Hot buttery biscuits, with fig preserves dripping inside, might persuade a woman to give her husband a second chance. Lord knows I have needed many of those second chances. I think Ed wanted me to know where I could find some figs the next time I needed some.

College students need second chances too. And professors like Ed know when to mix a little mercy with justice so that deserving students can make a fresh start. Without such kindness I would have never graduated from Auburn.

Second chances made it possible for Dean and me to stay together for a long time; we have now celebrated 58 anniversaries. We started our married life in student housing at Auburn in the summer of 1952. There was no room for a fig tree back then, but for more years now than Ed has been at Auburn, I have nurtured fig trees in my backyard. Those fig preserves, a healthy sense of humor, the Herculean patience of my wife, and a whole lot of grace have kept our marriage alive.

It would not surprise me to learn that Ed had "married" some of his figs to a few of Brother George's biscuits and served them to some of his students on a cold morning. This much I know: Ed is constantly looking for creative ways to "touch the clay" of his students' lives to help them realize their dreams.

Auburn University will continue to mold and shape young lives into useful citizens as long as there are teachers like Ed on the faculty.

Sharing stories and eating potato soup

X

Family fun is often the best kind of fun. The other night nine of us sat around the table telling funny stories while enjoying a meal of potato soup and sandwiches. What fun we had.

I know it sounds old-fashioned. Nobody cooks at home anymore it seems. The stove in many homes has not been hot for years. Everybody prefers to let somebody else do the cooking.

Some folks bring a pizza home and sit in the front of the television watching grizzly gruesome kill nine people. The only conversation occurs during the commercials when the couch potatoes complain that there is never anything worth watching anymore. Still they watch it, vainly hoping one day it will change.

Well there we were sitting around the table sharing funny stories and having another bowl of potato soup. No one seemed to care that the television screen was dark. Perhaps it was the pecan pie that kept us all together. Nobody wanted to miss getting a slice.

But I reckon the laughing we shared was the main thing that kept us together for well over an hour. Laughter is good for you. And like potato soup, laughter is healthy. We all need to laugh more that we do. It is good for the lungs, the brain, and one's general well being.

The laughing got started when one of my grandchildren described the hilarious breakfast some of us shared at IHOP. I stole the show by pouring coffee on my pancakes. Gales of laughter filled the room as I stared at my plate in disbelief, my face turning bright red.

Our waitress was a jewel. Though she shared the fun my family was having at my expense, she saved the day for me. She said, "Hey, you are not the first person to pour coffee on your pancakes. I have seen several people do that. It happens a lot." I felt better and left her a hefty tip.

What amazed me was that a simple thing like pouring coffee on pancakes could generate so much laughter. One dumb deed quickly improved the health of my entire family.

Our son Tim kept the laughter going by recalling a time last year when he decided to spend the night with his brother Matt and his wife Tammy. Tim found Matt at his church on a Wednesday night. Matt told him to go on to his house and he would join him later.

Tim found the home locked. Unable to get in, he walked around to the back yard and sat down in a lawn chair. The chair collapsed around him and he had to roll over on the grass to get free. Matt showed up an hour later, embarrassed to find his brother having to wait outside so long.

The only bed available for Tim was an air mattress positioned on an old bed frame. At 2 o'clock in the morning the air mattress suddenly went flat. Waking up, Tim tried to turn and get off the bed but at that moment the slats broke under his weight. His head and shoulders were trapped between the slats while his feet were dangling up in the air.

We were dying laughing as Tim described his predicament. Before he could free himself he said he promised the good Lord that he would stay at the Holiday Inn the next time he came to see his brother. Giving up on the bed and the air mattress, Tim chose to sleep on a couch in the family room. However, at 4 o'clock he was awakened by a dog licking his face. What a night! And all because he wanted to let his brother know he loved him.

Strange things happen to us in this life. We are not always amused by these experiences at the time. But in retelling such stories we find them a rich source of fun for ourselves and others. Add some potato soup and a slice of pecan pie and you have family fun at its best. But I still cannot believe I poured coffee on my pancakes! +

Dealing with difficult people

Sooner or later everyone must learn how to respond to difficult people. Fail to do so and they will make your life miserable. None of us can escape this assignment.

The place to begin is to admit that to at least a few people everyone of us is difficult to deal with. None of us is agreeable to everybody. As sweet as you may think you are, there is someone out there who finds you annoying. Your "sweetness" may be the very thing that rubs one of your acquaintances the wrong way. Have you not known a person who was so "nice" that it made you sick?

Once you can admit that, you can find a reasonable way to deal with troublesome people. You realize that there is more to this task than learning how to be patient with others. You understand that other people must struggle to put up with you. Growth can occur when this leads you to ask yourself, "What is there about me that irritates this or that person?"

Some people are like sandpaper – to you. God uses them to smooth off the rough edges of your personality. Such buffing hurts but makes you a finer person in the long run. Not getting your way about everything helps you mature. Good relationships require "give and take" for goodwill to exist.

Just remember that you are sandpaper to someone else! Each one of us is the grain of sand that produces a pearl in someone else's oyster. Forget that and you have an unbalanced view of yourself and others.

One pastor said his church was "the home of 3,000 warm and wonderful people and 2 or 3 grouches." That is a dangerous way to think. It conveys the assumption that the pastor and 2997 of his members were wonderful people who were spiritually superior to the three grouches. No way, Jose.

Often the people who complain are the catalyst for change. They can help us to see the truth about ourselves. Perhaps that is why the grouches are spread around; some of them are needed in every church – and in every person's life.

Some people are proud of their grouchy nature. They earned it by being hard to get along with and they work hard to maintain their reputation. They are intentionally disagreeable and enjoy being a fly in the soup of life. One man told me, "As long as I am on the board of this church, there will never be a unanimous vote on anything." He was true to his word. But being a "stick in the mud" is not a worthy achievement.

Our challenge is to guard against embracing an "us" and "them" attitude. We must constantly examine our own attitudes and behavior. Instead of pointing a finger at somebody else, we need to ask ourselves, "Am I a difficult person to my friends and associates?"

We need to admit that sometimes we are cantankerous ourselves, and willing to make life difficult for others. Such self-examination is, of course, extremely difficult, for most of us have 20/20 vision when it comes to seeing the faults of others. We can easily see "the speck" in our brother's eye but fail to see "the log" in our own.

The first step, then, toward dealing successfully with difficult people is to admit that sometimes you can be very annoying and offensive yourself. Once you can admit that to yourself, you can find a way to be more patient and understanding with those persons you find so disagreeable.

Beyond that you can develop the difficult habit of offering others more mercy than judgment. Harsh judgment of others always makes matters worse, while gentle mercy can open the door to a better relationship. Even if you are "right" in your assessment of another person's mistakes, you can never win another over through criticism. It only makes matters worse.

Finally, it helps to remember that you have not been sent into the world to "straighten everyone out." Some people appear to believe that their mission in life is to stand in judgment of the flaws of other people. Thus they make themselves, and everyone around them, miserable. Give that up for Lent.

Once you and I step down from the judgment seat, we can look for ways to offer the difficult person our understanding and friendship. Even if our offer is refused, the rejection does not make us less of a person. It could even cause the difficult person to realize that there is a better way to live. You can sleep better knowing that you did not allow the grouchy person to get under your skin and cause you to match their poor behavior.

Getting along with difficult people is not easy. It requires that you work at becoming less difficult to get along with yourself. If you work at it, you can improve your ability to get along peacefully with difficult people, and in the process become more fun to live with yourself. Remember too that there are no rewards at the end for having been obnoxious, rigid, and inflexible. Life is meant for nobler attitudes. +

Seven reasons to stop worrying

)(

Worry can kill you. Robert Frost said, "The reason worry kills more people than work is that more people worry than work." If Frost is right, then you need to find a way to stop worry before it kills you. So let me share seven big reasons why you should stop worrying.

One, worry is a waste of time. I read somewhere that worry is "like a rocking chair – it gives you something to do but it does not get you anywhere." That is a good analogy. Nothing is ever changed because we worry about it. The time you spend worrying could be used to accomplish some things worth doing. Use the time you have in positive, creative endeavors.

Two, worry depletes your energy. Worrying is hard work. It takes energy to keep it going. Worry uses up energy that could be spent in service to others. You have just so much energy on any given day; why waste it worrying about things that may never happen? Most of the things we fret may happen never happen anyway.

Three, worry can make you sick and ruin your health. Worry can render you helpless and put you in the bed. At the very least it can make you nauseous and miserable. If worrying is of no real value, does it make sense to continue worrying at the expense of your health? Mahatma Gandhi once said, "There is nothing that wastes the body like worry, and one who has any faith in God should be ashamed to worry about anything whatsoever." Well said, Mahatma.

Four, worry never stops bad things from happening. If an asteroid is going to hit you, it will hit you. Worry will not change its path. So why not enjoy what is good about your life until you get hit. Winston Churchill said the same thing with tongue in cheek: "When I look back on all these worries, I remember the story of the old man who said on his deathbed that he had had a lot of trouble in his life, most of which had never happened."

Five, worry robs you of today's joy while you are fretting about the troubles of yesterday or tomorrow. Worrying about what happened yesterday will not change a thing. Put your mistakes and heartaches to rest. Move on. Live in today's sunshine rather than yesterday's shadows.

Worry will not change what you said or what other people said. Criticism hurts. Tend your wounds and walk on. Stupid remarks cause lingering regret. Forgive yourself and walk away from your pity party. So you screwed up yesterday. So what? Everybody screws up now and then. Stop bemoaning the fact that you are a human being.

Make amends with people you have hurt – if you can. If you cannot, then you tried. You have no control over what other people choose to think or do. If you give them a chance to be at peace with you, then you have done all you can.

Six, worry keeps you from living one day at a time. "One day at a time, sweet Jesus"! That song says it all. Enjoy today, every waking minute. Squeeze the joy out of every day like you were squeezing the juice of an orange. Don't leave a drop. Get it all.

The person recovering from alcohol or drug addiction knows that the only hope for sobriety is to stay with the program one day at a time. But that formula works for all of life. It is futile to live in the past; it is impossible to live in tomorrow. All you have is today. Live it well. Savor its sweetness. Yesterday is gone and tomorrow may never come. Seize the day you have!

Look at life like Joanna Field did: "I used to wonder what life was for – now being alive seems sufficient reason." Yes!

Seven, worry is a sin so stop sinning and have faith. To worry is to refuse to have faith in God. Jesus said it plainly: "Do not worry." He warns us not to worry about our life, our clothes, or our food. Instead, focus on living to please God and trust your heavenly Father to provide the "things" you need. He knows what you need. He cares. You can trust him to take care of you.

Mary Crowley explains trust about as well as it can be put: "Every evening I turn my worries over to God. He's going to be up all night anyway."

Now I will ask all the experts, the philosophers, psychologists and preachers to sit down. I want the last word to come from a comedian we all loved. George Burns was funny but also wise. He said: "If you ask me what is the single most important key to longevity, I would have to say it is avoiding worry, stress and tension. And if you didn't ask me, I'd still have to say it."

So stop worrying so you can enjoy life to the fullest! +

27

Thanksgiving memories precious and painful

Thanksgiving memories are a mixed bag for most of us. Some are precious and some are painful. But life is like that and the challenge is to focus on our blessings instead of our problems. Somehow we must not allow yesterday's pain to rob us of today's joy.

My family was not wealthy. I was born on a farm when times were hard. My dad raised cows and hogs, grew cotton and corn, and always had a vegetable garden. I learned growing up that I had been born during the "depression." But I never thought of myself or our family as poor.

Because of dad's garden there was always food on the table even when there was no money. My siblings – three sisters and a brother – and I ate at a table that my dad built with his own hands. It was sturdy and big enough for the seven of us.

I still have that table. Recently my son Tim helped me put a new top on it. The legs need to be replaced but the table is still serviceable. I feel a strange sadness for families who raise children without eating together at a table. Back then there were no TV trays since there was no TV. I know things change, but I believe there is still value in sitting around the supper table together. It helps children feel they belong.

My siblings and I experienced accountability at suppertime. When my parents asked how things went at school, one of my sisters might pipe up and say, "Just fine, except I heard that Walter Junior (that was me) got a whipping by the principal today." My sisters had such good memories.

After supper my dad would take me out back to the wood shed. There he would remove his broad, black belt and give me a few licks. It was his way of encouraging better behavior at school.

O. M. Bratten, the principal, used a wooden paddle as his "board of education." He made a naughty student bend over a chair in his office. Then he would whack the rear end three times. To get a whipping at school was no dishonor to us boys. The only dishonorable thing was to cry, so we tried awfully hard to grit our teeth and convince ourselves that it did not hurt. We compounded our sin by lying, insisting to our friends that the whipping did not hurt.

After a paddling we were required to sit under the big clock in the school office. That was humiliating because everyone who came in and out of the office knew exactly why we were there.

The board was actually nothing compared to my dad's leather belt. There was no contest; that black belt left whelps on me that stayed sore for days. Does that mean that my dad had less compassion than the principal? I don't know. I do know that I never got a whipping I did not deserve. And I honestly believe the punishment caused me to change my behavior and pay more attention to the rules.

Let's get back to mamma's table. Mamma loved Thanksgiving and Christmas. She loved to serve a sumptuous meal especially on Thanksgiving Day. The bigger the crowd, the more she loved it. I can still see the bountiful feast she prepared, with turkey and ham, and always one of her specialties – toasted pecans.

Mamma always prepared pumpkin pie and potato pie. She fixed both for one reason: my brother liked potato pie more than pumpkin pie. The rest of us could eat two or three pieces of mamma's pumpkin pie, every slice decorated with whipped cream. It was not Cool Whip either; she whipped the cream herself.

But pie was not enough. Mamma never failed to serve ambrosia for dessert also. For the uninitiated, ambrosia is orange slices covered with shredded coconut, topped off with a cherry. Always tasty!

There was turkey, dressing, and cranberry sauce, along with a plate of ham. The vegetables were from daddy's garden and he never failed to remind us that he had grown the food himself. My parents believed in canning so we had an endless supply of lima beans, corn, tomatoes, okra, black-eyed peas, potatoes, onions, and green beans. Mamma and daddy took great pride in always having food on the table. Nothing pleased them more than to have their children, grandchildren, and great grandchildren come home for a Thanksgiving meal.

After lunch there was for many years the family ritual of covering mamma's green house with a thick plastic sheeting. I can still see my four sons climbing up on the roof, with some of their cousins, to pull that sheeting over the fragile glass roof. Dad had a gas furnace inside the green house so he and mamma could take care of their flowers through the winter.

The old green house was bull-dozed down after mamma and daddy died. It was just as well. Most of the windows were broken and it had not been used for five or six years. Dad was so proud of having built that green house for mamma. She loved to grow flowers, and she loved to give flowers to people.

Though mamma and daddy are gone now, and the old green house is no more, some wonderful memories remain. There are painful memories too – of broken relationships, broken families, and broken hearts. But I refuse to let these memories cloud my day or make me forget my precious Thanksgiving memories.

Thursday about 50 members of our family and some friends gathered again at the old home place. It is not the same. Our son Steve and his wife Amy remodeled it into an even more beautiful home. My wife and I did sit at a table in the same room where daddy's table once sat. We laughed and talked and shared precious members with my sisters Neva and Margie and cousins, Will and Gayle Anderson.

Painful memories were repressed, put aside for another day. Thanksgiving Day is a time for savoring precious memories and giving thanks that though life is indeed difficult, it is also good. +

Pastors hurt just like everyone else

Pastors hurt like everyone else. They cry too. And they can get so frustrated that they want to quit. If you did not know this, then you have never known a pastor well. Pastors are simply not immune to the problems that often overwhelm the rest of the human race.

Without a doubt there is much less stress in my life since I retired from active ministry. There is no longer the pressure to meet the high expectations of hundreds of people. And people have a right to expect excellent leadership from their senior pastor. As a part-time associate pastor I am content to leave many of the nitty-gritty problems of church life in the hands of the boss. I happily pray for him while thanking the Lord I no longer have to wrestle with issues that once overwhelmed me.

This week I came across the story of a pastor who ran away from home - not to get away from his wife but to get away from his congregation. This pastor spent three nights wandering the snow-covered mountains near his home. When he was found, he confessed that he was overwhelmed by life and just needed to get away.

Most pastors can sympathize with that pastor. Few clergy would deny that there are days when they too want to get out of Dodge. What may surprise us all, however, is how widespread this problem is with the men and women of the cloth. I was surprised to read that one psychologist said, "Pastors are the single most occupationally frustrated group in America." He went on to say that the demands upon pastors are so great that 30% to 40% of pastors eventually quit the ministry.

This clergy crisis is so extensive that one counselor said, "The incidents of mental breakdown are so high that insurance companies charge about 4% extra to cover church staff members when compared to employees in other businesses."

We are not surprised when other professionals quit one job and pursue another career. But pastors are "called of God" so we do not expect them to throw in the towel. Still, if we think about a pastor's life, we can understand why some pastors cave in under the pressure. People expect their pastors to be on call 24/7. They are expected to fill the roles of marriage counselor, crisis interventionist, personal confidant, and financial counselor as well as prophet and priest.

Such expectations thrust pastors into a constant whirlwind of stress. When the telephone rings, day or night, a pastor is expected to offer his help, rain or shine. To not be available would be a betrayal of his calling.

Some believe clergy are more stress-ridden that doctors, though the pressure on them is similar to that on pastors. But the doctor can walk away from terminally ill patients when he leaves a hospital room. The pastor, however, has emotional and personal ties to such persons and feels it necessary to suffer with them. It is well nigh impossible for him to "disengage."

Most pastors find it difficult to handle the pressure of living in a fish bowl, being scrutinized by their congregations and the community. Pastors may also increase the pressure upon themselves by believing they are expected to live a holier life than other people. A wise pastor will learn to "get over" this feeling and stop trying to "perform" for other people.

There is also pressure upon the pastor to wear many different hats. He is expected to be a spiritual "jack of all trades," able to leap tall buildings, serve as a counselor, business administrator, personnel manager, and still preach powerful sermons every Sunday.

One pastoral psychologist observed about pastors, "Their strong religious beliefs mean they won't kill themselves; they just spend their time wishing they were dead." That comment stings. I doubt the situation is that severe.

What is the solution? Pastors need to set limits for themselves. This will help them avoid burnout even if they are "on fire" for God. They need hobbies and interests other than church stuff. A support group can help. Meeting with a small group of men has been an enormous help to me over the years. A few close friends can help us come down off our pedestals and be real.

It has helped me to admit that I cannot do everything and need to concentrate on the things I can do best. Pastors need to remind themselves that they cannot help everyone nor can they be everything other people expect them to be.

Life became more fun for me when I finally understood that I cannot really solve the problems of other people. That is not my mission as a pastor. My job is to put people in touch with the One who can help them, the same One upon whom I am leaning for strength every hour. I try to remember every day that as a pastor I am simply a fellow struggler who can introduce hurting people to God. And they are more apt to believe me if I let them know that I hurt and cry too. +

The gift of understanding

Over 58 plus years of marriage my wife Dean has done a million little things for me. In earlier years I took her help for granted. In recent years I have been more conscious of the blessing she has always been to me. Actually I revel in the reality that somewhere, along the journey, we became inseparable partners in life.

Though I am grateful for all the little things Dean does for me, I realize now that the greatest thing she ever does for me is to give me her understanding. Over the long haul, nothing can beat the gift of understanding. In good times and in bad, it is the tonic we all need.

Elton Trueblood once said the best thing one person can do for another is to offer encouragement. Well, understanding is encouragement at its best. More than once, when I have been ready to give up on myself, my wife has rescued me with acceptance and support. Without her I would have thrown in the towel long ago.

Good friends also make a powerful difference with their understanding. Recently a good friend made me aware again how precious is the gift of understanding. His kind support at a difficult moment was heartwarming. It caused me to remember what it does to the soul when someone says, without criticism or a judgmental spirit, "I understand."

We are all alike when it comes to running to judgment. I am not proud of it but I have to admit that I am quite capable of being insensitive. Most of us are. We can hurt the feelings of our loved ones or best friends without meaning to do it. We can quickly condemn others when they have been foolish, careless, or thoughtless.

What we all need at such times is understanding – not condemnation. And when understanding is flavored with a bit of encouragement, then it is like a medicine that helps us recover. Failure, illness, loss of a job, divorce, or the loss of a loved one can trigger despair in the best of us. None of us is immune from the perplexities of life. When despair settles in, the last thing we need is for someone to come along with the stern advice to simply "stop feeling sorry for yourself." Such a comment only deepens the gloom that surrounds us like a fog.

What works wonders is for someone, especially a friend, to forget about their own struggles long enough to really identify with us, and to say genuinely, "I understand what you are going through." People who are not presently caught in the web of heartache are prone to suggest quick cures for others who are in trouble. We all need to remember these words of wisdom: "It is hard for a free fish to understand a hooked fish."

Recovery and healing take time. None of us can easily recover from harsh experiences that "cut us to the quick." We need time, and understanding, and the gentle caring of the significant others in our lives. People need people. Drugs are not enough. Even expert counseling is not enough. A new beginning is seldom possible without the aid of a few friends who understand.

The wonderful thing is that every person can participate in this kind of healing. We can not only benefit from the help and understanding of a good friend, we can also offer our own kindness and understanding to others around us.

Reading this, you may think you are an exception, that you are tough, self-reliant, and strong. You may be trying to convince yourself and others that you don't need anybody. You can make it on your own. Most likely you are wrong. Chances are you are made like the rest of us. Your best bet probably is to go ahead and admit you cannot make it on your own. Why? Simply because there is nobody walking around on two legs who does not need the gift of understanding.

So how do you find the understanding you need? Look around you. Find someone to whom you can offer your own gracious understanding, and give it. Stop harping about what's wrong and focus on what is right with the people near you. Just do it – give somebody the gift of your own understanding. First thing you know, it will come back to you, and sometimes from unexpected sources. The medicine you give may be exactly the medicine you need. +

Honeybees evidence of a beneficent Creator

X

I learned as a child to fear yellow jackets, wasps, and bees of all kinds. My cousins and I were not very smart. We thought we could outrun wasps and bees. So while the old folks were talking and preparing lunch for our family reunions, we declared war on some wasps and bees. We lost every time but proudly displayed the swollen signs of our courage.

Once we were severely reprimanded because one of our smaller cousins got stung about ten times. He danced around slapping at the wasps instead of running. That was the day we learned that some people are allergic to bee stings and can even die from repeated stings. We were stunned to discover that our fun could be so dangerous.

Though I consider myself rather adventurous, I have never had the slightest desire to harvest honey from a bee hive. There is no way I could be persuaded to put on a net and protective gear and retrieve honey while a thousand bees were crawling all over me.

My neighbor Jerry Smith is one of the brave souls who do not fear the bees. He has several hives in his backyard and sells honey to friends and neighbors. I love the honey he sells with the label "Vines and Hives." Somewhere I heard that honey produced within 25 miles of your home is more beneficial for you than honey from distant places. I like to think it is good medicine for my allergies. Jerry and Kay are great neighbors.

Honeybees get their name from the honey they produce. I had no idea there were so many different species of bees – about 20 thousand actually. I am amazed that someone took the time to count them. And I am even more amazed to learn that honeybees are the only living members of a certain tribe, the Apini tribe in the genus Apis. All of these bees produce and store liquefied sugar (honey) and build colonial nests out of wax secreted by the worker bees in the colony. The Apis bees are the true honeybees.

How honeybees make honey is simply marvelous. The life source of flowers and fruit tree blossoms is nectar, a clear liquid that is almost eighty per cent water but contains some sugars. In the Northern Hemisphere bees get nectar from the flowers of berry bushes, fruit trees, clovers, and dandelions. Honeybees use their long, tubular tongues to suck nectar out of the flowers, storing it temporarily in their "honey stomachs." The bees have two stomachs. One is their main stomach. The other is what some call a "nectar backpack" in which the bees store the nectar as they collect it.

What is amazing is that the honey stomach of a normal honeybee can hold about 70 milligrams of nectar. When this "backpack" is full it weighs almost as much as the bee does. So how many flowers or blossoms must a bee visit in order to fill its honey stomach? The answer the experts give makes me tired just to think about it: from 100 to as many as 1500 flowers!

The process is complicated. When the loaded honeybees fly back to the hive, they are greeted by worker bees that suck the nectar from the honeybee's stomach through their mouths. The worker bees chew the nectar for awhile as enzymes are reducing the sugars into a more simple sugar that is digestible for the bees. Somehow this process makes the sugar less vulnerable to bacteria while it is stored in the hive.

The worker bees spread the nectar throughout the honeycombs. This allows some of the water to evaporate, resulting in a thicker syrup or raw honey. While the water is evaporating the bees speed up the drying of the nectar by fanning it with their wings. That helps to explain why the bees always seem so busy. At some point the shift foreman of the worker bees decides the honey has just the right texture and calls for enough wax to seal off each cell. There the honey is stored until the bees choose to eat it. In a year a colony of these busy little creatures can eat up to 200 pounds of honey. Of course the average colony will have about fifty thousand honeybees!

But wait a minute! Honeybees eat honey? That's right. They make it for themselves, storing it so they will have food during the winter when the nectar in flowers is in scarce supply. That explains why the bees never seem happy when their honey is being taken away.

Bees are amazing. These flying insects live everywhere – except in Antarctica. Even though we steal their honey, honeybees do much good for us. They are pollinators. They help us grow the fruits and vegetables we eat. They provide us with honey. Honey is sweeter than sugar, does not spoil, and we eat it raw or cook with it.

Honeybees make propolis, a waxy substance that has some believe has medicinal value as an antibiotic, treatment for burns, and as an anti-fungal treatment. Propolis may also be used as a varnish for musical instruments made of wood; violins for example. It is used in some mouth-washes and sore throat lozenges. Beeswax is used in making candles, lubricants, cosmetics, and some pharmaceuticals.

Believe it or not, honey is an antibacterial agent and helps relieve some of our pollen allergies. Honey contains vitamin B6, thiamine, niacin, riboflavin, pantothenic acid, and minerals that are beneficial to our health.

Why do these flying insects exist? I have no doubt about the answer. Bees exist to give us a clue that there also exists a beneficent Creator who designed such things for our good. I am content to call this Creator our loving Father. The next time you enjoy a bit of honey on your toast, you might want to give thanks to the One whose love makes the honeybees possible. +

The right kind of people

Years ago I laughed at the antics of Tim Conway on television. His best comedic routines were those in which he imitated an old man shuffling along, moving one inch at a time. Now there are days when I realize I am that old man.

When I was young I took pride in my walking speed. I took long strides. Nobody walked at a faster pace. Friends would ask me to slow down. Now younger people walk past me as though I am standing still. At first it was surprising because in my mind I was moving along rather briskly. Then reality set in. I had to embrace the truth. I am slower than I thought.

But life is not over for those of us who are old and slow. We simply have to be careful about the people we choose to be around. Pessimistic people can make life miserable. Positive people who can see the funny side of life should be our first choice. The best of them are the ones who can laugh with us, not at us, when we take a spill. People who "lecture" us about every mistake can squeeze the joy out of life.

I like people with spunk, people who refuse to give up even when the odds seem against them. Somewhere I read a great story about Johnny Unitas, one of the most famous quarterbacks in NFL history. On his college team Unitas was a second or third string quarterback. In one game when his team got behind, he sent himself into the game to replace the starting quarterback. He did not have the coach's approval; he just ran on the field and took over. His leadership turned the game around, his team won, and the rest is history.

I love the story about the old woman who was looking for a space to park her bright red Mercedes. Noticing a place up ahead she moved slowly toward it. Before she could get there, a young man in another car darted in front of her to claim the parking place. She rolled down her window as the young man walked away and demanded to know why he had been so rude.

"Lady," he replied with a smile, "I guess that is what you can do when you are young and quick." As he walked on he heard tires squalling and looked back just in time to see the old lady ram her bright red Mercedes into the rear end of his car. Screaming at the woman as she got out of her car to await the police, the young man demanded an explanation. "Well, Sonny," she said, "That's what you can do when you are old and rich!"

That old woman is my kind of woman. She knew she was no longer young and quick but she was also realized she was not dead yet. She knew that older people still have a few options left. One of those options is to have fun until the end, to stay alive as long as you live. And it helps to be around people with plenty of spunk.

As we grow older we do lose some of our abilities. We suffer hearing loss, our eyesight dims, and our physical strength wanes. But we need not lose our enthusiasm for life itself. One woman said it this way, "I am 85 now. I can hardly hear thunder, and my eyesight is almost gone. But thank God, I still have my driver's license!"

That is the spirit we need to the end of life. As long as we can we must refuse to throw in the towel and give up. Once we give up, quality living is over. We may continue to breathe but instead of living we will merely exist. That time may surely come for many of us, but we need to put it off as long as we can. Somehow we must find the spunk to keep going even when our ears, eyes, knees, and backs are failing.

When I met Stanley Jones he was in his late seventies but he was still hale and hearty. His mind was still sharp; his wit remained keen. Brother Stanley was an immediate inspiration to me. He had spunk. Instantly I knew I wanted to be like him. He credited his good health and vitality to grace, gumption, and grass. By grass he meant the vitamin supplements he believed in. Gumption is what I call spunk.

Though I have not embraced Jones' love of health foods, I still like his plan. It is not a bad formula: grace, gumption, and grass. My plan is a bit simpler: grace and spunk. So if you find yourself in my situation-getting older and slower-you may want to a plan like ours. The "grass" may cost you a few bucks, but the grace and the spunk are free.

It takes spunk to choose to hang around positive people. But we do have a choice. We can walk away, even if it is at the pace of old Tim Conway, from the people who thrive on bashing us for every miscue. We can decide to spend most of our time with the people who help us get the most out of life.

Excuse me now. I am headed to the spunk store for a fresh supply.

+

The fascinating views of Martin Luther

)(

Martin Luther I have known for his theology and his role in the Protestant Reformation 500 years ago. Lately I have enjoyed reading for the first time about his personal life. His views on a variety of subjects are fascinating.

When an admiring woman told Luther she hoped he could live another forty years, he replied, "God forbid!" He said he did not want to live much longer mainly because the world was "full of nothing but devils." He had no use for physicians and insisted that "in God's name" he would eat "whatever tastes good to me." While I do not share Luther's disdain for doctors, I find in myself an enormous desire to "eat whatever tastes good to me."

In many ways Luther was a very practical man. If water, for example, was not available for a baptism, beer would serve just as well. During a time of drought Luther prayed earnestly for rain. And that very night some rain fell. When he was a young man games with cards and dice were forbidden. In later years he embraced such games as good exercise for the mind.

Luther scolded preachers for preaching scholarly sermons on lofty themes. He advised them to be simple and direct in preaching so that they could be understood by young people and children. As for the "learned doctors," if they do not want to listen, "they can leave." Luther once observed that "there are many fluent preachers who speak at length but say nothing, who have words without substance." Sadly it must be noted that such preachers were not limited to the days of Luther!

The German reformer had no patience with atheists of his day. Once he was asked about a citizen of Wittenberg who confessed publicly that he had not received communion for 15 years. Luther said that after a couple of admonitions he would declare the man excommunicated and to be "treated like a dog." He went on to say, "If the unbeliever dies in this condition, let him be buried in the carrion pit like a dog."

Someone asked Luther about a man who felt called to preach but whose wife had a haughty spirit and did not want to have a parson for a husband. What should the man do? Luther was asked. He replied, "If she were my wife I'd say to her, 'Will you go with me?' Say quickly,

No or Yes.' If she said No, I would at once take another wife and leave her."

When asked if a priest should give the sacrament to a man he knew to be a liar, Luther replied, "Do what Christ did; he gave the sacrament to the betrayer Judas."

One man questioned Luther about where God was before the creation of the world. Luther quoted Augustine whose answer to the question had been, "God was making hell for those who are inquisitive."

Luther had a way of saying things that were not always polite and spiritual. The forgiveness of his sins was terribly important to Luther. Good old boys could understand him well when he observed: "Apart from the forgiveness of sins I can't stand a bad conscience at all; the devil hounds me about a single sin until the world becomes too small for me, and afterward I feel like spitting on myself for having been afraid of such a small thing." Most of us have shared that feeling about ourselves.

Luther and his wife struggled in their marriage like most married couples. But he found great joy in his marriage. I found myself saying Amen to this tender observation by the reformer: "There is no sweeter union than that in a good marriage. Nor is there any death bitterer than that which separates a married couple. Only the deaths of children come close to this; how much this hurts I have myself experienced." Luther and his wife lost their daughter Elizabeth in her first year.

Dear old Martin had a delightful sense of humor. One evening he attended a wedding. Before the evening meal he advised the bridegroom to be content with the general custom and "be lord in his house whenever his wife is not at home!"

Martin Luther is surely one of the most fascinating figures in Christian history. Long before the term was coined, Luther was thinking and living outside the box. The need for such men continues. +

Conceit is an ugly attitude

An idiom is a common saying or phrase. Here is an example: "Money doesn't grow on trees." Some idioms hang around for years, being passed on from one generation to another. I have been thinking about one that must be several centuries old: "You are too big for your britches."

When we say a person is too big for his britches, we mean that he is conceited. He has an exaggerated sense of his own importance. A story about Mother Teresa reminded me of the britches idiom.

After participating in a workshop led by Mother Teresa, a preacher had the high privilege of having tea and a conversation with the famous nun. At one point as they discussed her ministry with the sick and dying, he asked her, "Mother, what is your biggest problem?" Quickly she replied, "Professionalism."

Momentarily speechless, stunned by her one-word answer, the clergyman said, "My jaw dropped. I had expected her to say something about the difficulties involved in trying to hold her community of nuns together. Or the difficulty of determining who would be her ultimate successor as the authority figure among the sisters."

Mother Teresa then explained her answer: "I have five sisters getting M.D. degrees and far greater numbers getting R.N., L.P.N. and M.S.W. degrees. But a funny thing happens. When they come back from their education, they are concerned about titles and offices and parking privileges."

How did she deal with their elevated sense of their importance? She said, "I take all of that away from them and I send them to the Hospice of the Dying. There they hold people's hands, and pray with them and feed them. After six months of that, they typically get things straight again and remember their vocation to be a spiritual presence first, and a professional presence second."

Those nuns were too big for their britches but Mother Teresa knew how to help them come down off their high horse and get it right.

Most of us delight in seeing a conceited person get his comeuppance. When someone gets knocked off his lofty pedestal, we usually say, "He got what he deserved." Sometimes when punishment seems slow to come, we may say, "Somebody needs to knock him (or her) down a peg or two."

We usually admire people for their skills but if they seem cocky, as though they know it all, our admiration fades in a hurry. That is why we love stories about famous people who "got it right" by having a humble attitude. Two such stories come to mind.

An American tourist visited missionary doctor Albert Schweitzer at his clinic in Africa. Schweitzer was world famous at the time. The tourist was shocked one morning to see Doctor Schweitzer pushing a wheel barrow across the grounds. "Why, Doctor Schweitzer," he said, "how is it that you are pushing a wheel barrow?" Schweitzer replied casually, "With two hands." Obviously Schweitzer did not have an unduly high opinion of Himself.

Even better is the story of George Washington Carver, the famous educator whose research led to the development of hundreds of uses of peanuts and sweet potatoes. An African American born to a slave family in Missouri, Carver one day at a train station in Atlanta heard a wealthy white woman say to him, "Boy, carry my luggage to the train for me."

Without a word Carver picked up the woman's luggage and placed it on the train for her. Cheerfully he accepted the dime she gave him and went on his way. His sense of worth was not diminished by the woman's failure to recognize and respect him as a distinguished inventor and educator. He was not puffed up by an inflated ego.

Humility can make even the most homely person beautiful. Conceit, on the other hand, is an ugly attitude that can make our lives miserable. It prevents us from being fun to live with. And worse of all, when conceit has wrecked our lives, and driven a wedge between us and other people, we have no one to blame but ourselves. It is never someone else's fault that you got too big for your britches.

The moral to remember when you start thinking you are hot stuff is this: You will live a longer, happier life if you don't take yourself too seriously. And conceit will not have a chance to split your britches. +

Our attitudes affect our health

There is little doubt that our health is determined to a great extent by our attitudes. Positive attitudes improve our health. Negative attitudes have a disease-inducing effect on the human body. This has been confirmed by the extensive research of many medical doctors.

The mind has an enormous impact on the body. Attitudes and emotions constantly affect the body for good or ill. It is for this reason that many books are being written about stress management. If we can become wiser about how to manage our lives, the result will be healthier living.

If you would like to research this subject I suggest you check out the book, Stress Without Distress, by Dr. Hans Selye, or the book by Dr. Brian Luke Seaward, Managing Stress: Principles and Strategies for Health and Well-Being.

Selye, for example, says that positive attitudes such as gratitude, praise, forgiveness, and joy will improve one's health. However, he points out, negative attitudes such as anger, resentment, jealousy, and hate have a debilitating effect on one's health.

Seaward insists that stress management and good health cannot be attained without consideration of the spiritual dimension of life. The soul needs a sense of inner peace in order to cope well with the demands of life. So it behooves us to learn more about the interaction of the spirit (or soul) and the body, as well as the mind and the body.

All of this raises many tough questions for which, I admit, I do not have all the answers. But that does not mean we should not seek answers. So consider this question: Can resentment cause a person to have arthritis? Surely in all cases the answer cannot be yes.

However, there is little doubt that negative attitudes (such as resentment) can weaken the body's resistance and make it more vulnerable to physical disease. Who says so? Well, for one, Dr. Loring T. Swaim does. I am indebted to my friend Maxie Dunnam for introducing me to Swaim.

Swaim, a physician, specialized in orthopedics for 50 years. At Harvard Medical School he lectured on arthritis for 20 years. In his book, Arthritis, Medicine, and the Spiritual Laws, he documents many case histories of persons who were set free from crippling diseases by surrendering resentment and bitterness and the submission of their self-will to God.

Swaim became convinced that negative attitudes toward others can be "causative" of rheumatoid arthritis and other organic diseases. And if not causative, then negative attitudes will definitely weaken our resistance and make us more vulnerable to disease.

If these medical doctors are right, then we might want to examine ourselves – now and on a daily basis – to see if we are allowing negative attitudes to make us vulnerable to disease. Some conclusions seem quite logical:

If I am harboring resentment toward someone, and that resentment is robbing me of my good health, then I need to stop resenting that person or anyone. After all, my resentment is not hurting the other person; it is hurting me.

If I am unwilling to forgive someone for what they have done to me or said about me, and my unforgiving spirit is making me vulnerable to physical disease, I need to forgive that person. If practicing forgiveness can contribute to my good health, then I need to get busy forgiving others.

If bitterness and jealousy are endangering my health, I would be a fool to go on being bitter and jealous.

If hatred toward someone is making me so angry that "I cannot see straight," then I am paying a huge price – my good health – for the privilege of hating another person. The price is too high.

Good health is one of our most valuable assets. Surely not one of us is so foolish as to continue being negative if by becoming positive in our attitudes and emotions we can enhance our health. As in so many areas of our lives, it is simply a matter of choice. And the choice we make will affect our health for good or ill. +

il talking to myself.

46

If God is out there why doesn't he speak?

My friend Banks Herndon is a devout Christian. He prays every day. Yet like most believers he sometimes wonders if there really is a God who hears our prayers. Recently, while riding in his truck in a pasture, Banks actually asked God why He never speaks directly to him. He got no answer, no word from the Lord.

A few hours later as he was reading his email he came across a lesson I had written. I had raised the same question he asked God: "Is anybody there, listening when I pray? If there is a God why does he stay hidden? Why doesn't he speak up when I call out to him?" Startled, Banks thought, "That is exactly what I asked God this morning!"

In sharing this experience Banks said, "Then, with a clear voice, though not audible, God reminded me of rainbows and roses. He had spoken. He had answered my prayer with a direct communication to me. God really does hear!" Banks concluded by thanking me for my lesson.

What Banks did not realize was that God had also spoken directly to me—through Banks' email. Let me explain. I spend a lot of time writing, and even more time trying to think of something relevant to write about. Not many people ever respond, pro or con, to my writing. People are busy with their own lives. I understand that.

But at age 78 I keep pondering the question, "When are you going to stop writing these lessons and columns and spend more time with Dean and your grandchildren?" Most of the time I think, "Well, Lord, all good things must end sometime, so I guess I will put down a final period at the end of this month, or maybe I will wait until the end of December." I hear Him saying, "I will love you just as much after you stop writing as I do now."

About the time I decide to hang up my saddle and turn the horse into the pasture, someone like Banks writes to say "You are making a difference." It seems like God orchestrates these messages to encourage me to continue writing. I may be wrong of course. I could be imagining God doing this. There is no way to prove it. I will never know for sure. But it does seem "just like God" to make such things happen.

Do people really hear God speak? I believe so. I know I have, though never in an audible voice. But I have met a few people who claim to have heard God speak audibly. Estelle Carver said she did. She was a brilliant English teacher and a devout disciple of Jesus. I sat at her feet several times in a Bible study.

One day she said, "When I was 12 years old, I heard God speak. He called my name. It was an audible sound that deeply moved me to surrender my life to Jesus." Later someone asked Estelle, who was 75 at that time, if she had ever heard God speak again. Her reply was awesome: "No," she calmly replied, "One time was enough. I was so deeply stirred by His Voice that I have never needed to hear Him again."

Unlike Estelle I have never heard God call my name -- audibly. I have concluded that, for me, it was enough to have met a woman who had heard Him call her name. Her devout and holy life was evidence enough for me.

Have I heard God call my name in the chambers of my heart? Oh yes! Many times in my walk with Christ I have heard Him whisper in my heart, "Walk through this door that I have opened for you." Over the years I learned to walk ever more quickly through those doors -- and every time He has blessed me far beyond my deserving.

Seldom has such a decision been easy. Each time I have had to give up what I had in order to receive what He was about to give me. But that is the nature of authentic discipleship; we must relinquish what we have in order to receive the new blessings God wants to give us. If our hands are wrapped too tightly around what we have, then we have no open hands to accept God's new gifts.

My friend Joe told me about a young man who, having lost his job, went to see an old preacher. With clenched fists he said, "I've begged God to say something to help me, preacher, why doesn't God answer?" The old preacher's reply was barely a whisper. The troubled young man stepped closer to the preacher saying, "What did you say?"

Again the preacher spoke in a soft whisper. The young man moved closer but still could not understand what the preacher was saying. Finally, with their heads bent together, the young man heard the old preacher say, "God sometimes whispers," he said, "So we must move closer to hear him."

Surely we would all be wise to listen more intently, in the midst of the loud voices of our world, for God's gentle whisper. To hear we must get closer to the One who is the "Word" of God. The sweetness of His Voice will make us wish we had learned to listen sooner. +

We saved money by staying home

A vacation usually involves travel. But with the price of gas so high, travel these days is very expensive. So this summer my wife and I chose to stay in Alabama for a week's vacation. It was a good decision. We saved money and had a wonderful time.

Of course we were tempted to escape the hot, dry weather of the hottest August on record in Alabama. But we reasoned that had we left the state we might have had worse problems than the 105-degree heat wave that dragged on for weeks.

We love Minnesota but had we gone there we might have been on that bridge that fell in the river.

We love Texas and Wisconsin but had we traveled to either state we might have been drowned by the flood waters that ravaged those states.

Mexico is nice but had we planned a getaway to Cancun, we would have arrived just in time to get blown away by Hurricane Dean. I knew from day one that I did not want to tangle with a hurricane named Dean.

All of the above justified our decision not to leave Alabama. So on our first day we traveled only a hundred miles from home, having reserved a room at Mt. Cheaha State Park near Anniston. Actually the address is Delta, Alabama, but only the folks who live there have ever heard of Delta.

Why Mt. Cheaha? We reasoned that people go to the mountains to find cool air and Mt. Cheaha is the highest point in Alabama, 2,407 feet above sea level. Well, you guessed it. There had been no cool air at Mt. Cheaha. Like everywhere else in Alabama, it had been hot and dry there for weeks.

That is, until we arrived! It rained both days we were there and in the late afternoons we enjoyed a nice cool breeze. We sat on a bench overlooking the vast Talladega National Forest and admired the natural beauty of Alabama's highest pinnacle. We held hands and talked of bygone days when the kids were small and the stress of life was such a struggle. We gave thanks for the peace of more pleasant days that is ours now, having come through "so many dangers, toils, and snares."

We enjoyed Mt. Cheaha so much that we decided to move on to another state park – DeSoto Resort State Park near Fort Payne. Again we traveled less than a hundred miles. This time we rented a cabin in the woods and found it delightful. The cost for a cabin was the same as for a room in the park lodge, and less than the price of a night's lodging in a nice motel.

The DeSoto Park is near one of our favorite getaways – Mentone. We have enjoyed staying there in more than one bed and breakfast inn, though the cost nowadays is a hundred dollars or more. By staying in a cabin for several days we saved some money, eating several simple meals in the privacy of our little cabin. Cold cereal is hard to beat most any morning as long as I can find a couple of cups of coffee.

Our last stop was completely unplanned. We got off the busy highways and decided to ride awhile on state highway 25. That took us through Wilsonville and soon to a wonderful little town we had never visited before – Columbiana.

Having noticed on the map that there was a museum in Columbiana, we decided to check it out. Much to our surprise the museum housed a fine collection of George Washington memorabilia. While there we inquired if there were any bed and breakfast inns nearby.

Our gracious hostess first said no; there were none in Columbiana. Then her face lit up as she remembered that a new one was about ready to open for business just down the street. She called on our behalf and gave us directions to the stately DuBose home on East College Street.

There we met Andrew and Diane Moore who kindly invited us to be their first guests in the beautiful home they had been renovating, off and on, for five years. They did practically all the remodeling work themselves. The result is most impressive – a marvelous old home built in 1889 completely restored, sharply decorated, and ready for guests to enjoy its exquisite Victorian flavor. An appetizing breakfast in such surroundings, along with gracious southern hospitality, can make the heart sing.

The Moores, who live upstairs, have named their bed and breakfast the Columbiana Inn though the sign for the front yard is still at the print shop. Six bedrooms, each with a private bath, are available for use. Each room is equipped with cable television and wireless connectivity.

One room, with a private entrance on the front porch, is called

"The Visiting Parson's Room." We stayed in the lovely bedroom next to it but the room has not been named yet. Diane laughed and said she might call it "The Backslider's Bedroom." We thought that was a great idea. We are experienced backsliders.

Soon we hope to return to Columbiana, one of Shelby County's best kept secrets, and enjoy another night in the little town's newest and only bed and breakfast, the Columbiana Inn. Our time there was a delightful way to conclude our money-saving, stay home in Alabama vacation. +

Joy, the reward of serving on a team

Ж

A great part of the joy of living comes from the privilege of serving on a team. Human beings are not designed to live as hermits. We need other people. Evidently our Maker had this in mind when he created us.

A baby needs a mother. A mother needs a husband to help her raise her children. Growing children need role models. Adults never outgrow the need for mentors. As one sage said, the person who has no mentor but himself is the mentor of a fool. People need people to live life at its best.

In every arena of life people serve together on teams. The concept of teams is not exclusively that of athletics. Teachers, politicians, doctors, nurses, accountants, attorneys – they all work in teams. People who sell cars and trucks work for dealers as a team.

People used to wonder why my friend Hugh Dean Fuller in Opelika was so successful at selling cars. I learned his secret. Every morning, six days a week, he met with his sales force at 6 a.m. He taught them the art of selling cars. He built a fire under them to be the best team in town. His enthusiasm was contagious. When people came out to look at a car, his team was ready to seal the deal.

Business leaders are looking for team players. They know that products can be built best (and sold best) by a team of people who are committed to a common goal. Most athletic teams cannot function effectively unless the players learn to work as a team. Persons who are "glory hungry" are not team players.

As children most of us felt the pain sometimes of not being selected when teams were chosen. It hurt to be one of the last persons picked to serve on a team.

Growing up we gravitated toward the people we identified with, or the people who wanted us on their teams. Many of us had a "gang" we ran with. We belonged. We were accepted. We felt comfortable with people who felt comfortable with us.

My mother insisted that I take voice lessons. I did. I joined our high school Glee Club. We were a team. But I still remember the embarrassment of being kicked out of the Glee Club for being a smart elec. I deserved it but it still hurt.

I went out for football in the tenth grade and made the team for three years. But my skills were limited. So limited that I spent most of my time sliding up and down the bench hoping the coach would call my name. I still have a couple of splinters embedded you know where.

Then the Friday night came when Coach Phillips called my name to start at right tackle. I could hardly believe it. That was one of the greatest moments of my teenage years.

This fall my grandson Jake is wearing my old jersey number (79) on the Macon-East Academy football team. He will play tackle, mostly on offense. Up in the stands I will be wondering if his heart skips a beat like mine did so many years ago. Of course at 280 and 6 feet three inches tall he gets to play on the varsity as a tenth grader, something that eluded me.

As a pastor I learned early on that I could not succeed as a "lone ranger." Realizing that I needed a team, I was blessed many times with the high privilege of serving with men and women who worked together as a team. Any preacher worth his salt must surround himself with a good team.

In Pensacola for seven years I had a wonderful team at Richards UMC. Some of those teammates are still friends.

At Trinity United Methodist Church in Opelika I served with one of the greatest teams any church ever had. We had our problems. None of us was perfect. But we found a way to work as a team through thick and thin. Years later we remain the best of friends.

Now I am the old guy on a great team at Saint James United Methodist Church in Montgomery. I get to cheer for a super senior pastor and encourage the others on our staff to function as a team at all costs. Our mission is too important not to work together.

A beautiful thing happens when a congregation can see with their own eyes that the pastor and his staff love one another. To see such love in action makes the people glad they belong to the greater team that is their own church.

Come to think of it, any team in any arena that learns the art of loving one another is usually a stronger team. Perhaps that is the unspoken goal of teamwork – to practice the kind of love that wants the best for one's teammates. That's when our acronym for TEAM means "Together Everyone Achieves More." After all, there is no "I" in the word team.

Serving on a team can inject joy into your bloodstream – especially if it is the right team and each player has the right spirit. +

Anticipation a precious human emotion

There are many things in life that most of us take for granted. Take rain for example. We did not think much about it until this summer. Now even the atheists in Alabama are thanking God for a little rain.

A faucet with running water is more precious to me after spending two weeks in Zambia. Even though Victoria Falls is located in Zambia, there are millions of people there who will live their entire lives without ever having running water in their home.

In America we have plenty of rest stops available to us when traveling. But during our seven-hour bus ride from Lusaka to Livingstone we passed through several communities where there was no public restroom. After enduring several "close calls," some of us will never again take public toilets for granted.

Conveniences we take for granted are luxuries in other parts of the world. Even a brief visit in a third world country makes you keenly aware of that.

In addition to things we take for granted, there are certain aspects of the human spirit that we ought to pause and give thanks for. We are capable of many emotions such as anger, despair, affection, apathy, fear, guilt, pity, hysteria, hate, shame, pleasure, and the greatest of all, love. Normal people experience all of these and more.

Today I want to give thanks for the wonderful capacity of anticipation. That surely is one of our most precious human emotions.

When we define the word anticipation we must use words like "enthusiastic" or "excitement" to explain what we mean. Anticipation is an emotion that often involves pleasure while expecting some desired event. It is somewhat like hope though hope seems like a more sober emotion. Excitement is another name for pleasured anticipation.

Of course anticipation can also involve anxiety or irritation. We may be worried as we anticipate a coming event or we may be frustrated at having to wait.

Anticipation can cause some people to become happy and excited as they wait for something to happen. Other people can become ill or frightened as they begin to imagine bad things occurring, things that may deny them the joy they are longing for.

To anticipate something wonderful happening, and not have it occur, can be devastating. It can bring on such grievous disappointment that we despair of life itself. But to anticipate a great blessing, and receive it, can result in unspeakable joy.

In these hot, dry August days I am using the emotion of anticipation to add joy and excitement to my life. I am eagerly anticipating the beginning of the football season. I am excited about getting to cheer for my grandsons Jake and Josh as they play for Macon-East Academy. Jake is a tenth grader playing tackle and wearing my old jersey number 79. I can see him picking up a fumble and running it all the way back for a touchdown!

I want my Opelika Bulldogs to become state champions this fall. I see them beating Prattville in Birmingham. And I'll be on the sidelines!

I am eager to yell "War Eagle" until I am hoarse and watch the Auburn Tigers become national champions. They did it 50 years ago and it is time for my Tigers to do it again.

I am anticipating a full house at church one Sunday this fall. One of these days before I pass on, my head usher will walk up to the pulpit and tell me with a broad smile, "Preacher, we have standing room only this morning!" It will happen. That day will come.

We have a great choir at our church. I am anticipating that one Sunday they will sing so wonderfully that the congregation will give them a ten-minute standing ovation. And the people in the pews who are not clapping with delirious joy will be shouting "Hallelujah" and dancing in the aisles.

One more thing: I am anticipating that one Sunday soon I will preach so well that there will be a stampede at the altar as people come forward to get right with God. I can already hear someone shouting, "At last, thank God almighty, the preacher is on fire!"

You owe it to yourself to enjoy the emotion of anticipation. Pleasured anticipation is not just for the young, old folks! Take a deep breath and believe that wonderful things are going to happen in your life this fall – and get busy making them happen! +

Perseverance necessary for life's journey

ϫ

No matter which path you choose, life is tough. There are obstacles on every road. Sooner or later the difficult journey we call life will demand perseverance from every traveler.

The people who succeed in life are those who learn to "stay with the program." Those who fail make a habit of starting something and quitting. Quitters never win. Winners keep getting up after being knocked down, again and again. They are the people we all admire – those who refuse to quit the race no matter how many times they fall.

This was brought home to me by my friend Dan Morris, a pastor in Navarre, Florida. Dan told me about a man I had not heard of before, a pilot named Cal Rodgers. Only eight years after the Wright brothers invented and flew the first airplane, Rodgers became the first person to make a transcontinental flight. A pioneer American aviator, he flew a Wright Flyer from Long Island, New York, to Pasadena, California, in 1911.

My research confirmed that the feat by Rodgers was indeed a marvelous example of perseverance. Rodgers' goal was to make the coast to coast flight in less than 30 days so he could claim the $50,000 prize offered by William Randolph Hearst. He missed his goal by 19 days but his perseverance made him an American hero. He survived crashing his plane 39 times! Each time a ground crew rebuilt the plane. When he finally landed in California the only parts of the original plane that were left were the rudder and the drip pan!

Rodgers kept going despite severe injuries suffered in crashing his plane, the "Vin Fiz." (He named his plane after a grape drink made by the company that sponsored his flight.) Even though Rodgers was thrown from the "Vin Fiz" 15 times in crash landings, broke both legs, an ankle, a collarbone, and cracked several ribs, he refused to quit. He persevered to the end.

A sad footnote to this story is that less than a year later Rodgers died in a freak accident. While making a test flight in Long Beach he flew into a flock of birds, causing the plane to crash into the ocean. He died of a broken neck, becoming the 127th airplane fatality in aviation history. The inscription on Rodgers' gravestone reads: "I endure. I conquer." His willingness to endure earned him a place in the Hall of Fame.

Most of us will not attempt such daring feats during our lives. Nevertheless our success will depend upon our willingness to persevere in spite of the barriers we must hurdle. The perseverance required of us is not a moment of miraculous courage but daily stepping up to the plate and doing the right thing over and over again.

Along the way all of us are tempted to give up. The price may seem too high to pay. We see others cheat and get away with it. They manage to have things we want so we begin questioning our decision to always do the right thing. Maybe cheating does not matter as much as we once thought. Others get away with it so why not join them.

The problem is that every morning you have to deal with that fellow looking back at you in the mirror. He keeps gently nudging you to never give up doing the right thing. That man in the mirror can help you stay on the right track if you will listen. An unseen Person is coaching him to help you stay on the straight and narrow.

My friend Dan Morris nails it when he says that what we all need is "a holy toughness that God hammers into the soul." If we allow God to use his hammer on us, somehow we will be able to persevere when the going gets rough. And at the end of this journey called life, we will have the enduring joy of winners instead of the awful pain of losers. +

.

Uncle Dave's toys

When I was a child I loved to visit the home of my mother's uncle, Dave Johnson. I suppose that made him my "great" uncle, but I never called him that. He was simply Uncle Dave, who lived with Aunt Pearl in a beautiful home on a hill a few miles from our home. We lived in a more modest home near a swamp on river bottom land.

Though I never had the feeling that we were a poor family, I did understand that Uncle Dave was "rich," and he was an old man. He owned a lot of land and his home was quite fancy, much nicer than ours. His home had the first spiral stairway I had ever seen but he frowned when we slid down the banister.

It was fun to visit Uncle Dave because he loved children. He always had a couple of mechanical toys hidden in his desk. He liked to surprise us by letting us look at them while they performed. I can still hear him laughing as we watched with amazement a little clown or some other toy dancing around on his coffee table.

My favorite was the monkey that walked around in a circle while beating on a drum. Children were not allowed to touch the toys. When Uncle Dave felt we had enjoyed them enough, he would put them back in the safe haven of his great oak desk. This, I would learn years later, was his way of insuring that the toys would be available for the next child's visit. I did not understand as a child why I was not allowed to play with the toys. Now I understand.

Imitating Uncle Dave, I have bought a number of toys to use in amusing my own grandchildren. The one the children liked the most was a small Santa Claus that cost me the grand sum of five dollars. Only Santa cannot enjoy his battery-powered walk anymore. One of my grandsons broke off one of his feet, so all Santa can do now is ring his little bell as his arms go back and forth. I should have been as wise as Uncle Dave and kept old Santa out of harm's way. It seems that some of the little rascals not only enjoy seeing a toy move, they also enjoy fixing it so it cannot ever move again.

When Uncle Dave's grand old home burned, it was a sad day for me. It was not easy to drive by and view the smoldering ashes of a home that held so many happy memories for me. I wondered if his toys, still hidden in his oak desk, had also perished in the flames. How delightful it would have been to take my grandchildren to visit Uncle Dave's place. What stories I could tell them about his toys and my exciting trips down that polished banister! But the old home and Uncle Dave are gone. They are but fading memories of a childhood that seems so long ago.

Still I am here, and there are children aplenty. If I am willing I can take the time to surprise them with a toy and create a sparkle in their eyes like Uncle Dave did for me. But to do it I must be willing to stop being a stuffy old adult long enough to see the world through a child's big eyes.

My friend Bubba helps me do that. Bubba, you see, is more than a talking bear; he is like a member of the family now. Ever since I gave Bubba Bear to my wife one Christmas, old Bubba has helped us entertain the grandchildren. My wife never tires of squeezing Bubba's hand so she can hear him talk. That just may be the best forty-five dollars I ever spent.

So I reckon as long as there are Bubba Bears and dancing Santas to buy, we will keep on doing what we can to make the eyes of little children – and grandmothers – sparkle with joy. Whatever else we may face on life's journey, it remains true that a little fun will help the medicine go down no matter what your age. +

Thanksgiving a time to count your blessings

There are many old gospel songs rambling around in my brain but none more lovely than "Count your many blessings." At Thanksgiving time no song says better what we should all be doing.

This old favorite says: "Count your many blessings, name them one by one, and it will surprise you what the Lord has done." How true that is.

In spite of our illnesses, disappointments, and heartaches, we are all blessed far beyond our deserving. So as you prepare to celebrate Thanksgiving, do yourself a favor and make a list of your blessings.

See if you don't agree that some of our greatest blessings are the simple things that make life good. As you read over my list, make one of your own and share it with your family and friends. Perhaps, like me, you won't have to look far to see some of your finest blessings.

Outside my office window I am sometimes visited by a beautiful red bird that sits for a few minutes on the azalea bush. He rests for a minute, as though to say hello, then flits off on his daily routine. I would not want to cage him, but for a few moments he is mine to enjoy. I've named him Pete, after a good friend named Pete who is also a blessing.

My surroundings are a constant blessing. In our home my study is called "the Happy Room." We bought this home from Don and Gale Shaddix who had decorated this bedroom for their little boy, Alan. The wallpaper is bright and cheerful, with hundreds of colorful balloons that are being released by dozens of "Teddy Bears." I find it hard (though not impossible!) to be grouchy and unpleasant in "the Happy Room."

Outside "the Happy Room" window, in our front yard, are several dogwood trees. I did not plant them, but because someone else did, I can enjoy them. Dogwood trees are handsome in two seasons -- the spring with their gorgeous blossoms and in the fall with their bright red berries. Whoever first began encouraging Opelika residents to plant Dogwood trees has surely been a blessing to us all.

Sometimes when I am working at home on Fridays I can witness another marvelous blessing. That is the big garbage truck that comes by faithfully to empty our garbage cans. These "sanitation engineers" are a wonderful blessing to our community. We do well to salute them and thank them for the important service they render to us all. This is one blessing we could not do without!

We are surrounded by great neighbors. It is no small thing to have neighbors who know your name and care deeply about you. That is one of the inestimable values of having friends and being friends. My neighbors are a blessing I gladly count.

Two other friends in our neighborhood are a couple of big cats who patrol our back yard. The cats do not belong to us, but like Pete the red bird, I claim them as our own when they stroll through the yard. What they eat I do not know, but since living here we have never seen a rat or any mice. So I have an idea we owe that blessing to the cats who, though never together, seem to enjoy our yard.

Thanksgiving for many of us will include a good meal on Thursday. As we enjoy it we need to remember that there are many hungry people in our community and our world who will not sit down to a feast. While we thank God for what we have, we may also want to ask how and where we could give a helping hand to others.

Thinking about simple blessings, we can surely thank God for the lowly pecan. My mother taught her family to love toasted pecans and every Thanksgiving I always look for some. What a great day's work the Lord did on the day he decided that his people would enjoy the blessing of pecan trees! Count your blessings -- it will help you have a great Thanksgiving! +

I love a story that touches the heart

Jokes that bash the college we love to hate are commonplace. When I hear one, I enjoy it but quickly forget it. Most are not worth remembering.

But I love a good story that touches the heart. I wouldn't swap a touching story for a dozen funny jokes. When I began preaching, back in the dark ages, I had the idea that every sermon should begin with a good joke to grab everyone's attention. For a few years I kept a joke file close at hand, jotting down new ones on 3x5 cards.

Then I discovered that the truth is funnier than jokes. So I began telling the truth instead of jokes and found that my preaching was more effective. The reason: people could identify with the real-life experiences I shared.

It was not easy at first. I was apprehensive as to how people would react to their pastor admitting his shortcomings. Some did indeed question my admission of fear and frailty. One woman responded with a haughty tone in her voice, her nose stuck up in the air as she said, "I am very disappointed to learn that my pastor has such problems!"

What I began to realize is that preachers cry and bleed like everyone else. The difference is that some admit it while others refuse to admit it, choosing instead to hide behind a smoke screen of piety.

Frankly I began to enjoy being a real human being instead of pretending to fit the stereotype which many people have created for preachers. It was refreshing to have people say to me, "I know how you feel because I have faced that same problem in my own life."

So I found new courage to relate to people as a fellow struggler, rather than as one whose faith was so strong that there were no more problems. To my great delight this resulted in a new depth of relationships with people from all walks of life who, like me, were looking for help, hope, and encouragement to meet the harsh realities of life.

Not long ago I lost myself once again in the self-obsessed fog known only to the workaholic. When I am in that fog I become insensitive to the needs of my wife and often make stupid comments which scramble our relationship.

Stunned by the estrangement which follows, I begin to sort out my priorities anew, realizing for the one-hundredth time that my wife's love is infinitely more important to me than the mountain of work I have been climbing.

When I swallow my pride and admit this to her, she is always graciously forgiving and willing to renew our relationship with tenderness and understanding. Once again I realize that the things that matter most are the things that make life worth living. One more time I resolve to put first things first so that I can avoid the pain that has been ripping my heart out.

If reading this, you feel like saying I've been there and done that, then you are on my page and you know what I mean. You also know the profound difference between a joke and a story that touches the heart. Given the opportunity you and I could sit down and share our hearts with each other for hours, truly identifying with the hurt and hope that throbs within us, longing to be known and understood. And, best of all, neither of us would ever think of sharing a joke, because it is so much more refreshing to embrace the truth about ourselves. +

I'm tired of being sick

Life is filled with many mysteries. One that intrigues me has to do with sickness, and the issue of praying for the sick. What can we expect of God when we offer prayers for the healing of those who are sick?

Some people are reluctant to pray for healing. They say, "God knows I am sick; if he wants me well, then he will heal me."

Others say, "There are some things God will do only in answer to prayer, so we should ask him in earnest prayer to heal those who are sick." The implication is that unless we pray, then the sick person will remain sick or die.

When I was six years old I almost died with scarlet fever. My parents told me years later that they prayed all night for God to save me. One doctor gave up on me. Another doctor tried a new drug and I recovered. Did the medicine save me or did God heal me? Or did God guide the second doctor to know what drug would save my life?

In her mid-thirties my wife had major surgery. Her recovery was not certain. The doctor said to me, "Your wife is a very sick woman." I prayed for her healing. A few days later my wife's countenance suddenly changed. She appeared radiantly healthy and was soon discharged from the hospital. Her doctor seemed surprised.

Weeks later she shared with me a remarkable experience. Alone in her hospital room she realized that she was quite ill. For more than 10 years, since childhood, she had lived a very sickly life. Quietly she began to pray for health and strength so she could go home and tend to her children. She prayed, "Lord, I'm tired of being sick all the time."

That afternoon the weather was hot and muggy; the window in her room had been raised slightly to let in some fresh air. As she prayed, her eyes closed more from fatigue than reverence, she suddenly felt the presence of someone in the room. Opening her eyes she was surprised to see no one there, yet the sense of someone present remained.

Moments later she was aware of a gentle breeze flowing across her bed. The cooling air seemed so refreshing, as though her whole body was being invigorated. It felt so good, she said, "it was as though someone had tenderly wiped my brow with a cool washcloth." She closed her eyes again in prayer, confident now that there was someone with her, someone whose presence gave her a deep sense of peace.

Telling me about this experience later, she said that for several minutes the cooling breeze and the calming presence remained in the room. Then as quickly as it had come, it was gone. But she felt different. For the first time in weeks she felt good. She knew that she was well, physically and spiritually. She believed that her health had been restored and there was now a quiet peace in her spirit. She knew beyond any doubt that she had been visited by God himself.

Later that day her doctor, quite surprised and pleased by her sudden healthy radiance, informed her that she could go home the next day. As you reflect on this experience of one woman, what questions come to mind? Was this a dream? Was she confused by medication? Would she have recovered any way, whether or not she had felt the breeze and the presence? Or perhaps, why did God heal her and allow others to die in that very same hospital?

I have no pat answers to all these questions. I have more questions than I have answers. But I can tell you that I had been her husband for years while my wife endured continual sickness. All of our married life she had been a very sickly person.

I can also tell you that I have been her husband since the day of her hospital "visitation," and for more than 40 years she has enjoyed amazingly good health.

After all these years, can we explain what happened? No, but we still believe that sometimes God heals the sick in answer to prayer. And sometimes he does not. Why some and not others, we do not know. Mysteries remain. But that does not stop us from celebrating the good things that happen when Someone enters our lives like a gentle breeze on a hot and muggy day. +

Overload - the disease for which many of us are seeking a cure. We did not mean for it to happen, but it did. We stretched ourselves like a rubber band trying to wrap ourselves around so many good things that our wagon got loaded.

Pain, pressure, and frustration- these unwelcome neighbors moved into our lives, pushing us to the breaking point. Emotionally drained, we want somebody to listen to us cry, scream, or shout, "Stop the world! I want to get off!"

What we really want is not a way out, but a healthy life filled with contentment, simplicity, and balance. We get sick of being stressed out, hurrying all the time, tired to the bone, and worried about everything under the sun. We want someone to lead us out of the jungle of stress, fatigue, and anxiety.

One solid answer was offered recently by the CEO of Coca Cola Enterprises, Brian Dyson. Speaking to university graduates at commencement exercises, Dyson talked about the difficulty of juggling priorities.

He invited the graduates to imagine life as a game in which they are juggling five balls in the air - work, family, health, friends, and spirit. It's hard work, he said, to keep all of these balls in the air at the same time.

Dyson invited his audience to understand that work is a rubber ball. When you drop it, it will bounce back. But, he said, "The other four balls- family, health, friends, and spirit- are made of glass." Drop one of them and "they will be irrevocably scuffed, marked, nicked, damaged, or even shattered. They will never be the same."

Even Pepsi lovers will agree with the Coke executive's wisdom. Work makes a poor god; worship it and you miss the true joy of living. There are some things that are simply more important than work - the other four balls that Dyson insists tend to be broken or damaged when dropped.

If our goal is balance in life, we must learn to treat family, health, friends, and spirit as balls, or priorities, made of glass. Of them we must be willing to say, "Fragile: handle with care."

Brian Dyson may have read with profit the excellent book, **Margins**, by medical doctor Richard A. Swenson. In his book Swenson offers a prescription for overloaded lives which he calls "margin."

"Overload," Swenson says, "is not having time to finish the book you're reading on stress. Margin is having time to read it twice." What we need, he says, is to stop pushing ourselves beyond our limits so we can gain margins of energy reserved for the unexpected demands of life.

As we face the continuing challenge of juggling our priorities every day, listening to people like Dyson and Swenson can help. Here is my attempt to merge their advice into a sentence to remember:

"If you expect to solve the problem of overload, be careful not to drop the glass balls!" +

Memorable maxims meliorate mental muscles

Maxims are truths that are shared daily by all people everywhere. They are rules of conduct by which we learn to live safely and wisely. Here is a good example: "Always look both ways before crossing the street."

Parents teach maxims to their children for their own good. Adults share them with one another to express in a few words a fundamental principle of life.

As we journey through life most of us "collect" favorite maxims which we enjoy sharing with others as evidence of our mental prowess. Lately several friends have shared favorite maxims with me so that I could add them to my collection. I share them with you, along with a few others I have picked up here and there.

Bill Rawlinson shared these two:

"Bad news does not improve with age."

"To err is human; to really screw up, use a computer."

Jennifer Jones gave me this one: "Bibles that are falling apart belong to people who are not."

Jack Smollon offered these:

"It is easier to get older than it is to get wiser."

"It's hard to make a comeback when you haven't been anywhere."

"Only time the world beats a path to your door is when you're in the bathroom."

Coach Spence McCracken likes these:

"The good you do will be forgotten tomorrow. Do it anyway."

"Give the world the best you have and chances are you will get kicked in the teeth. Give it anyway."

"What you spend years building can be destroyed overnight. Build anyway."

Julia Child said this: "I was 32 years old when I started cooking. Until then I just ate."

Here is one from C. S. Lewis: "Nothing that you have not given away will ever really be yours."

Carl Sandburg offered a brief sentence which he said is always appropriate no matter what the circumstances: "Life goes on."

Some one-liners contain helpful humor even though they may not qualify as a genuine maxim:

"He who laughs last thinks slowest."

"Lottery: a tax on people who are bad at math.'

"Consciousness is that annoying time between naps."

"I used to have a handle on life, then it broke."

"All generalizations are false, including this one."

"Puritanism is the haunting fear that someone, somewhere may be happy."

"Hard work has a future payoff. Laziness pays off now."

Albert Einstein said: "Great spirits have always encountered violent opposition from mediocre minds."

Kennon L. Callahan is one of my mentors and one of my favorite authors (www.josseybass.com). His books about "The Twelve Keys" have blessed churches all over the world. Ken's ideas have greatly impacted my life. Here are a few of his clever sayings:

"Idealism is the ancestor of cynicism. Vision is the antidote to idealism."

"Wisdom is common sense in living life."

"Grace is slow to speak. Advice is quick to answer."

"Grace knows there are many ways to do something. Advice always knows the right way to do something."

"Blessed are those who can laugh at themselves, for they will be frequently amused."

"Life becomes more complex when we try to do everything ourselves."

"You can steer a ship only when it is underway. When it sits dead in the water, you cannot steer it."

"Excessive helpfulness breeds excessive behavior."

"Excess breeds excess. Balance breeds balance."

"Memory is strong. Hope is stronger."

"The devil has a device called resentment with which he tries to convince Christians they are really doing the will of God."

"The art of life is to discover one's mission. The joy of life is to serve well."

"Our wants are the devil's way of distracting us from what is really important in life."

Finally I will offer one of Callahan's finest sayings to end all of this:

"The more I listen, the more I learn. It is extraordinary what people can teach you when they are given half a chance."

Amen! +

A reality check I sorely needed

✕

A friend and I were having lunch in a little German café in Pensacola when the completely unexpected happened. I don't remember what we ate that day but I will never forget my friend's gentle but shocking rebuff.

He had listened patiently while I rehearsed once again my story of having been treated unfairly by some of my "Christian" friends. He had heard all the gory details from me before, more than once. I had been hurt and I wanted sympathy from my friends, even though the hurtful event had been history for two or three years.

My friend interrupted me and remarked bluntly, "Walter, don't you think it is time you stopped talking about all that garbage and get on with your life?" The silence was as stunning as the look on my face. Staring into his eyes, I was surprised at my own reaction. I felt no anger at his candor. Instead I realized that he had said exactly what I needed to hear.

The time had come for me to stop blabbering about the past and move on. I broke the silence finally, admitting soberly, "You are right. I need to stop complaining about all that mess, and I will stop right now." I thanked him for speaking the truth in love to me. It was a reality check which I sorely needed. And I did stop bellyaching about that hurtful experience. In days to come I even found it fun to realize that I could control my tongue and resist the temptation to bring up all that stuff again.

It was a good lesson for me. It helped me to realize that I am in charge of the garbage of my past. I can choose to retrieve it and stir in it again and again, or I can let it go. Letting it go frees me to enjoy the present and anticipate a bright tomorrow.

I love it when I say to a friend, "How are you doing?" and he replies, "I can't complain." Can't complain? Of course he could complain. But he chooses not to complain!

In these days observe how people love to gripe. Nine out of ten people, whether strangers or friends, will grumble about how hot it is, about the drought, about how long it has been since we had a good rain.

Yes, it is hot. Yes, we need rain. But remember, it could be worse. And no amount of complaining will cause it to rain or to cool off.

When we feel compelled to squawk about our problems, we can give ourselves a reality check. We can stop complaining and start counting our blessings.

Is it costing a lot to cool your home during the summer months? Instead of whining about that big AC bill, take a look at your gas bill and rejoice. My gas bill will be very low until we get some cold weather. Think also about all those families in Kosovo who don't even have a home or milk for their babies. Our plight could be worse, far worse. Heat, after all, is a seasonal thing. Stick around -- it will get cold again before long. And that is not something you can say about a certain place where the fire will burn forever!

So we do well to heed this good advice: Stop complaining and move on with your life! Only then can we become fun to live with! +

When everything seems to be going wrong

X

Ever have one of those days when everything seems to go wrong? You know, one of those days when you find yourself saying in despair, "I should have stayed in bed!"

Sure, you do. We all do. That's a part of living a normal life because none of us is perfect. You may demand that other people live perfectly around you, but you know deep down that they cannot do that anymore than you can. So we have to learn how to cope with our own failures and those of others.

Crazy things happen to the best of us. Take, for example, the woman in London whose cat got stuck up in a tree. Unable to talk the cat down, she called the fire department. Soon four experienced, helpful firemen were on hand, with a truck and a big bucket. One of the firemen was hoisted up in the bucket and was able to rescue the cat. The woman expressed her gratitude by inviting the whole crew inside her home where she served them tea and biscuits. After a few minutes of good food and fellowship, the firemen climbed back into the fire truck, and backed out of the driveway, waving to the grateful woman.

She watched in horror as the fire truck backed over her cat and killed it. So for the frustrated and now sad woman, and the firemen, it was one of those days. The kind we all have from time to time.

Take preaching, for instance. A preacher can go to great pains to tell a marvelous story only to have someone come up to him later with a question that ruins his day. Bill Hinson tells about the country preacher who quite eloquently retold the creation story with a little homespun twist to it. God, he said, made Adam out of mud and then leaned him up against a rail fence to dry. But a wry old farmer raised an objection. "But preacher, if Adam was the first man, where did the rail fence come from?" Redfaced, the preacher replied icily, "It's questions like that that just ruin religion." I know how that preacher felt. Every preacher does. What can we do to salvage our sanity on those days when everything goes wrong? Two things at least are helpful to me.

One, never surrender to pessimism. When things go wrong, pessimism knocks on your door and wants to move into your mind. Best advice I know is to refuse to let the old rascal in. Run him off with a broom.

Two, never give up on optimism. Even when the milk is spilled, find a way to laugh about it. Clean up the mess and go on. Life is too short to part company with optimism.

So get another cat if you've got to have one. Buy some more milk. Tell yourself that the floor looks cleaner where the milk was spilled. Smile and pick yourself up and move on. As bad as the day has been, tell yourself it could have been worse!

I heard about a football coach whose team kept having losing seasons. He was a good coach and his teams almost won every game. But a fumble or an interception kept snatching victory out of their hands.

Somehow the coach remained positive. He refused to complain. Asked how he kept his spirit up, he shrugged his shoulders and said, "I'm the kind of guy who, if I fell in a mud puddle, would get up and feel in my pockets for fish." Now that is a winning attitude even when your team is losing!

So keep your chin up. Don't give in. Believe in yourself and keep wearing a smile. Say, don't I smell fish frying in your skillet? Fix up a pan of cheese grits and enjoy yourself! +

January first is a fresh start

)|(

The cynic will be amused by my response to the first day of the New Year. He will say, "Relax, Walter; it is just another day on the calendar. It has no more significance than any other day of the year."

Not for me. No sir. January first is a beautiful day. I love it. I welcome it because it gives me a fresh start. Life has a way of grinding us down. A new beginning helps us deal with the unending misery of life.

A new start enriches every aspect of life. Without new beginnings most marriages will not last. Mine would have ended in chaos and sadness years ago had my wife and I not forged at least forty new contracts along the way.

Why so many fresh starts? That is easy; nobody is perfect. We all make mistakes. We say things we wish we had not said. We do stupid things without thinking. I am the President of that Club. I have a gift for saying something dumb and before I have finished the sentence I am already asking myself the question, "Why in the world did you say that?"

Making stupid comments can cost you the friendship of people you care about. I believe I have several good friends but every one of them has had to forgive me for saying something asinine. I think it is true that a real friend knows who you really are, so my true friends know that on occasion I can be a royal jerk. They know – and understand – that I can screw things up about as quickly as anyone.

Friendship can survive only where people are willing to forgive one another and start over. Those who expect perfection from themselves and others wind up with few friends, if any. Only those who learn how to say, "Please forgive me," will have lasting marriages or friendships.

In the area of physical exercise, I have spent my life starting over. I paid forty-nine dollars for a Charles Atlas muscle-building kit when I was a teenager. I wanted muscles so the girls would admire me. I wanted hair on my chest. So for a few weeks I exercised like crazy. If only I had kept at it, I might look like Arnold Schwarzenegger now and be governor of California.

But alas, I did not. However, I do keep forgiving myself and starting over again. Once again I am planning to ride my stationery bike for

40 minutes a day and take better care of my aging body. Yes, I will probably quit again, but soon I will make a fresh start and go at it again. I am simply unstoppable – about starting over again.

In the matter of reading for personal pleasure, I am making a new beginning. I have made a list of five books I plan to read in the new year. I started to say January, but at my age I need to stop putting undue pressure on myself. Other people are good at pressuring me so there is no need for me to help them. When I finish those five books, I will start on a new list. After all, I do want to watch a few good football games.

My new woodwork shop is almost completed and the use of it fits into my plans for the New Year. My dream is to spend quality time in the shop with my sons and the other men in our family – as well as several of my friends. This represents truly a new beginning for me – a new hobby that can make a difference in my life.

One genuine value of January first is the opportunity to put the past behind us by burying old wounds, lingering guilt, and hurt feelings. If we allow it, the pain of the past can dog us to the grave. But we can break the chains that bind us if we are willing to do one thing: Get Over it! Put it out of your mind. Stop regurgitating your hurts. Flush it all. Be done with it. Move on.

Once we are willing to get over the stuff that enslaves us, we can move on. We can make a new start and nobody can rob us of the fun we will have in celebrating our freedom from past pain and failure.

January first is not merely a new month and a new year. It is a glorious new day – a chance for a new beginning wherever you need a fresh start. Do not let the sun go down until you have started over putting first things first. +

The touch of another hand

Most nights after we go to bed my wife will rub my forehead for a few minutes. It is sort of a ritual which I enjoy and encourage. I don't mind admitting that the touch of her hand makes a difference in my life.

Of late our society has discouraged touching. The result is that fewer of us are willing to put an arm around someone, especially someone of the opposite sex. That bad word, "harassment," hangs in the air around us. We are scared of appearing to do the wrong thing even though our intentions are noble.

I submit that this trend is robbing us of something that people need. We all need to be touched physically now and then by our friends. We need more than to have our hearts touched; we need the tender touch of a friend who understands. Who is so stiff as to say that a pat on the back is not often helpful? I know some people want to keep others at arm's length, perhaps because they have been hurt and don't wish to be hurt again. I understand that.

There are those who insist on being proper and impersonal. They wear a sign on their faces that says, "Keep it strictly business, folks; don't get close to me." They let us know that you had better keep your distance. Six feet is fine. But human beings are not stiff boards. We are not trees or fence posts. We are living beings who need to experience warmth, acceptance, and genuine friendship from the people with whom we live and work.

I remember when my boys became teen-agers that they stopped hugging the old man. One of the boys said as I offered to embrace him, "Let's just shake hands, Dad." He had become self-conscious about hugging his parents in front of his friends. What he seemed to be thinking was that hugging was a bit silly now that he was so "grown up." I patiently endured his reaction but how I thank God now that when this big son comes to see me, a handshake will not suffice. He grabs me in a bear hug that blesses me - after I am able to start breathing again!

I understand that hugging is practiced selectively by most of us. Most men are quicker to hug the pretty women than they are the less attractive gals. And some people don't get hugged because they send out signals with their eyes that say, "Watch it, buddy; hug me and you'll get a knot on your head!" I understand all that. We are different. We react differently to affection.

But still I remain convinced that we need to find a way to save the art of touching. We need each other. An occasional hug to express joyous affection and friendship need not be understood as a desire to go to bed with someone.

As for me I remain a champion of hugging. We need to find appropriate ways to express true affection for one another. Especially since there are times in our lives when the touch of another hand can make all the difference in the world in the survival of our hope.

A bumper sticker asked, "Hugged your child today?" Good question! How about a bumper sticker that says, "Hugged a friend today?" So if you have not received your quota of hugs today, stop by. No matter what the stiffly polite people say, I like hugging. +

Why some pastors are so frustrated

Ж

Recently a 55-year-old pastor ran away from home - not to get away from his wife but to get away from his congregation. According to news reports, the California pastor spent three nights wandering the snow-covered mountains in San Diego County. When he was found, the preacher confessed to authorities that he was overwhelmed by life and just needed to get away. Most pastors can identify with this pastor.

Few of us would deny that there have been days when we too wanted to get out of Dodge for a spell. But, frankly, I am surprised to learn what a serious problem this is among clergy. One psychologist, Richard Blackmon, was quoted as saying, "Pastors are the single most occupationally frustrated group in America." Blackmon says the demands upon pastors are so great that roughly 30% to 40% of pastors eventually drop out of the ministry.

Commenting on this clergy crisis, H. B. London, Jr. noted that about 75% of religious leaders go through a period of stress so great that they consider quitting. London said, "The incidents of mental breakdown are so high that insurance companies charge about 4% extra to cover church staff members when compared to employees in other businesses."

It is not difficult to understand why many pastors cave in under the pressure. Pastors are, after all, expected to be on-call for a congregation 24 hours a day. At any moment they are expected to fill the roles of marriage counselor, crisis interventionist, personal confidant, and financial counselor. Such expectations thrust pastors into "a constant whirlwind of stressful events." When the telephone rings, day or night, a pastor is expected to offer his help no matter how weary he or she may be. A pastor must be constantly ready to answer a call for help.

London feels that clergy are more stress-ridden that doctors who are ministering to the terminally ill. While the doctor can walk away from the situation when he leaves the room, the pastor, unlike other professionals, "normally has emotional links and personal ties to those being helped and suffers with them."

Pastors also feel the pressure of living in a fish bowl and being scrutinized by their congregations and the community. Pastors sometimes feel that they are expected to live a holier life than other people. There is the added pressure upon the pastor to wear many different hats. He is expected to be a spiritual "jack of all trades," able to leap tall buildings, serve as a counselor, business administrator, personnel manager, and still preach powerful sermons Sunday after Sunday.

Pastoral psychologist Archibald Hart recently observed, "Their strong religious beliefs mean they won't kill themselves; they just spend their time wishing they were dead." That is a rather stinging observation about today's clergy! I hope that the situation is not as bad as some think.

What is the solution to the problem? London and others recommend that pastors set limits for themselves so as to avoid burnout. It helps to have hobbies and interests outside of the church. A support group of fellow pastors can be a great help. It has often been a help to me.

It will help also for the pastor to admit that he cannot do everything and to concentrate on the things he or she can do best. It helps me to remind myself often that I cannot help everyone, nor can I be everything that other people expect me to be. I know that I am a very, very fortunate pastor. While I am sometimes frustrated with the heavy demands upon me, I never feel like quitting, and I am constantly thankful that people need me. Even more, I am thankful that I finally understand that I cannot really solve the problems of other people, as much as I might want to.

My job is to put people in touch with the One who can help them, the same One upon whom I am leaning for strength every hour. It helps to realize that you are not God; you are just a fellow struggler who can introduce God to hurting people. When the pressure mounts in my own life, I try to remind myself to do the best I can and leave the rest to God. He is very good at renewing my peace, relieving my pressure, and restoring my sanity. +

A great mystery

During my 18th year I began to nurse the notion that God wanted me to become a preacher. At first I was afraid to tell anyone. Then I told my pastor and a few close friends. My pastor affirmed the idea and, in the same sentence, scared me to death. He invited me to preach in our church the next Sunday night.

Quickly I discovered that being called to preach, and writing a sermon, are two different things. I had no idea where sermons came from. And I was certain I did not know how to write one. Fear seized me and held me in its terrifying grip.

My saintly grandmother, Neva Carmichael Johnson, came to my rescue. She had given me a book of "Gospel Sermons" written by great old evangelists like Billy Sunday and Dwight L. Moody. Not knowing any better, I picked out a sermon on "Happiness" and preached it in church that Sunday night.

Why "happiness" appealed to me I don't know. Perhaps it was because I was simply happy to have something to say. In later years I derived some humor from remembering that my very first sermon was a good one, so good it was already in print!

But I realized that night that I had a lot to learn. For one thing I was so nervous that I could not stand still. My friends thought it was neat that I moved around a lot. What they didn't know is that my knees were knocking so that I could not stand still. Then I read most of the sermon. I am embarrassed now to think about what an ordeal it must have been for the congregation - to endure a nervous, 18-year-old boy standing in the pulpit reading someone else's sermon.

What is worse, there was not an honest person in the audience that night for everyone took the time to tell me what a good job I had done and how proud they were of me. I must admit that I enjoyed their lying, but now I realize that most of them probably went home muttering under their breath, "Lord, if the future of the church depends upon the likes of that poor boy, then heaven help us!"

For the next few years, as I pursued my education at API, now Auburn University, I was invited occasionally to preach at small country churches. Gradually my preaching got better, for I discovered books of sermons written by Clovis Chappell and Charles Allen. I learned later that Clovis and Charles were also "helping" many other preachers with their sermons.

Three years of seminary training convinced me that I could, and should, learn how to write my own sermons. So gradually I learned how to weave my own life experiences into my sermons. Only then did I learn the power of being real, of sharing the raw truth about my hurts and feelings, my fears and dreams.

This taught me that sermons are more helpful when people can identify with the preacher, when they can feel that the preacher understands personally how the scriptures impact their lives. The listener wants to be able to think, "The preacher understands how I feel and what I am going through." Effective preaching accomplishes that rapport. You know it has happened when someone says after listening to you preach, "Pastor, you have been reading my mail."

In these days I don't succeed in preaching such sermons every Sunday but that is always my goal. One of my friends remarked to me one Sunday, "Some of your sermons are better than others." I got a good laugh out of that as I thought, "Thank God, because some of my sermons just taxi down the runway and never get off the ground." Every preacher knows the pain of having preached such a sermon.

When the preaching is especially poor, the agony of the listeners is almost unbearable. It is little wonder that some people go to sleep - in self defense. As one who has now been preaching for half a century, one of the great mysteries of life is that people can sit still long enough to hear someone else preach a sermon.

On behalf of my fellow preachers, I ask your forgiveness for those times when our sermons bore you out of your mind. And I thank you for your patient willingness to believe that now and then you will hear a sermon that will be worth your time.

Do know that without your love and encouragement none of us could ever find the nerve to stand up and preach Sunday after Sunday. Your encouragement fuels in us the hope that God may be willing to take the poor thing we offer him and use even it to touch someone's heart. +

Sayings my father left me

My father influenced me in many ways, not the least being the many phrases of speech which I inherited from him. So now I often think of him when I make comments that I first heard from his lips, sayings that over the years have become part of my vocabulary.

When he wanted to emphasize the truthfulness of something he said, he would often conclude with the remark, "If that's not true, there is not a dog in Georgia!" The implication is clear: the statement is true because everyone knows there are plenty of dogs in Georgia.

I have no idea where my dad first heard those words. Most likely it did not originate with him. Perhaps it was his own dad, an uncle, or an acquaintance. Whatever its origin, it found lodging in the recesses of my mind years ago.

Now and then I even use this remark in a sermon as a humorous way of inviting my audience to know that I truly believe what I have just said. It is a way of underlining an affirmation of truth, or making a statement with "bold face" speech.

Family members and close friends have a way of sharing, unconsciously, their vocabulary with us. We learn from each other. We pick up words or phrases that appeal to us and add them to our own reservoir. Over the years we get into the habit of using certain words or phrases in everyday conversations. The use of these expressions become characteristics of our unique personalities.

When someone is telling me a story, for example, and I realize that the other party is expecting me to do little more than listen, I find myself saying repeatedly, "You don't mean it." As I become conscious of having used that expression several times, I begin to alternate it with a one-word response – "Really." Then if the story is exceptionally long, I begin to look for an opportunity to say something like, "Well, thank you for sharing with me, but I really must run along now."

I laugh when I remember an old friend who, becoming exasperated with a friend who would not stop talking to him, kept raising a finger to indicate that he wanted to reply. Finally, when his friend kept ignoring his signal, he raised his whole hand and said with emphasis, "If you would please put down a period, I have something I would like to say!"

But such an abrupt remark usually brings to an end any significant sharing since the talker feels rejected.

There are a few people of my acquaintance who seem to need nothing but an ear, into which they are willing to pour endless words without any response from me. These persons probably imagine they are having conversations when actually they are doing almost all the talking. It can hardly be described as a conversation if one party does 99 percent of the talking.

Along the way we all pick up meaningless phrases which we use habitually. One such phrase is "You all come to see us." If everyone we had spoken those words to showed up at our house one afternoon, we would probably have a stroke. What we usually mean by that phrase is this: "This casual contact with you today is about all I really need."
I cannot remember if my dad ever said, "Have a nice day," as a parting comment to someone. But I picked that phrase up from someone and use it a lot every day. Perhaps it is simply one of those socially acceptable remarks that makes our daily speech polite.

One remark I am trying to stop using is the very common phrase, "Have a good one." A good what? I suppose it a shorter version of "Have a good day." But while pleasant, it means little more than the overused "See you." Come to think of it, I never remember my dad saying "See you" or "Have a good one."

So I reckon I have someone else to blame for all these sayings that have slipped into my vocabulary. And if that's not the truth, there is not a dog in Georgia! +

Into every life some rain will surely fall

Every Sunday somebody tells me "a good one." A good story, a good joke, or an encouraging quote. So I go to church expecting to hear at least one or two good ones.

Last Sunday was no exception. One man asked me if I knew how severe the drought in Alabama had been. So I asked him how bad it had been. He said, "This bad: the other day I saw two grown bull frogs in a ditch and neither one of them had ever learned to swim!"

Not bad. It was good for a laugh. Laughter is always helpful in church, for strange things happen in church. People get angry with each other sometimes over the least little thing. One woman asked another woman to stop wearing a certain perfume; it made her sneeze in church.

A woman came storming up to me one day to insist that I tell a certain mother to stop disturbing church by taking her little girl to the bathroom. I resorted to my "grin and bear it" attitude by saying, "I'll ask the Lord to help me figure out what I can do about it." That means, "I don't plan to die in that ditch." And usually the Lord passes on such stuff also.

My wife did have a solution for this problem when our boys were small. She told our sons to go to the bathroom just before worship. Then she reminded them that they would not be permitted to leave the church service. I think she didn't want our boys to disturb the folks who were sleeping while I was preaching. If during church one of our sons said, "Mom, I've got to go," she simply said, "No, you don't; go ahead and wet the pew. After church I will wipe it up with this towel in my purse." None of our boys ever wet a pew.

Troubles do develop in churches because they are made up of people, and people have problems. Sometimes they disagree about things. Now and then people can choose sides and manage to split a church wide open. That is always sad when it happens.

I hear about a church in Tennessee that split up over the issue of which foot should be washed first in the foot-washing service. Now I have heard there is a church in the Volunteer State called "The Left Foot Baptist Church." I guess they are the folks who quit wanting to worship with the folks who wanted to wash the right foot first.

Honest, I am not making this up -- and the story did say that it was a

Baptist Church. I suppose it could have been a Methodist Church, but my guess is that the Methodists heard about this dispute and decided against the practice of foot-washing in church. If so, they were wise. It is just not smart to fight about some things.

Trouble in church reminds me of that old saying, "Into every life some rain will fall." How true that is. Life is not always sunshine and roses. Sometimes we all have to deal with storms and thorns. Life is not easy and my guess is that God did not mean for it to be easy.

Troubles do come, and troubles do go. Like the storms, they don't last forever. In the midst of them our faith is tested. And somehow we become stronger through the testing. We learn to decide what is truly important. We often learn that none of us is always right, and at times we find that we must admit we have been wrong. It usually takes that for a breach in friendship to be resolved.

The Japanese talk about an attitude they call the "bamboo perspective." They see the need to learn to bend, but not break, under the pressures of life. Unity with other people is usually not possible unless we are all willing to bend a little in our attitudes. Divisiveness thrives when no one is willing to bend.

We might learn a lesson from a story I heard about a brand new fifty dollar bill. The preacher held it up in church and asked if anyone wanted it. Every hand went up. Then he crushed the new bill in his hand as if he were wadding up a piece of paper. Again he asked if anyone wanted it. Once more every hand was raised. Next he dropped the $50 bill and ground it into the floor with his shoe. Now the bill was dirty and wrinkled. Does anyone still want it, he asked. As every hand went up again, the people realized his point. The bill was not worth any less because of the dirt or its wrinkled condition. It was still worth the same as a brand new bill.

What is the point? If people throw dirt on us, or damage our reputation, our worth is still the same to God. If we stumble into mistakes, or make decisions of poor judgment, our value remains the same to God.

The lesson? Surely God wants us all to learn to think as he thinks, to love as he loves, and to forgive as he forgives. When we are willing to do that, even imperfectly, we may save God the grief of seeing his churches divided. In the meantime, a little laughter over a few "good ones" will help us all. +

What is special about Shell, Ecuador?

Everybody does not agree with the idea of sending "mission work teams" to other countries. Here are some of the responses people have made to me:

"It costs a lot of money to fly to another country, so I believe it would be wiser just to send the money you would spend for travel to help people there."

"Going on a mission work team is simply an excuse for taking a vacation in a foreign land."

"The host missionaries cannot do their normal work because it takes so much of their time to entertain their visitors."

"The people in other lands are happy with their way of life. We have no right to interfere with them and try to make them accept our American way of life."

Well, I disagree. From what I have seen, and experienced personally, participating in a mission work team is usually a life-changing experience. That is the testimony of dozens of people who have traveled with a team to Mexico, Costa Rica, Haiti, Paraguay, Ecuador, Honduras, Brazil, and Africa.

Not long ago I traveled with a team of 15 persons to Quito, then made our way to work for five days in a remote place called Shell, Ecuador. Though the work was tiring we felt a strange sense of joyous satisfaction about the help we had given some very poor people.

We returned with a few souvenirs and 15 bags of stinking, dirty clothes. In Shell we worked with our hands in the rain and sunshine of that beautiful country. At night we enjoyed fellowship and meals prepared by our missionary hosts who serve there with MAF, Missionary Aviation Fellowship. Our primary host was Sandy Toomer, a pilot who lives in Shell with his wife Trish and their children Harrison and Sarah.

What did we do to justify the costs of going? (Our round-trip fare was $608.) We completed the construction of a school room which will be used for teaching children. Other work teams were there before us; we simply continued the work they had begun. Still other work teams will follow us to expand on our work. It is truly a cooperative venture.

We encouraged the people who are serving there. Everybody needs encouragement, even the wonderful people we call missionaries. We affirmed them all--men, women, and children-for the good work they are doing, at considerable sacrifice. They have given up many of the daily conveniences we take for granted in order to serve people who are unbelievably deprived.

We assured the missionaries of our continuing support. They can remain there only if people back home support them with money and prayers. Our church family takes great delight in supporting the Toomers.

Why an honor? Listen for five minutes to Sandy and you understand. This summer he and other pilots there have flown over a thousand children out of jungle villages into Shell and other bases to attend Bible schools. Sandy knows that anyone of these children can grow up to become a responsible Christian person. After all, the instructor who taught Sandy flying lessons had once been an impoverished kid in a remote island of the Philippines - until a pilot like Sandy found him and guided him into a new way of life!

But Sandy uses his airplane in many other helpful ways. Routinely he flies sick people out of jungle villages to secure medical aid. Many people would never see a doctor without this help, although Sandy does sometimes fly medical personnel into remote areas to treat the sick. It means a lot to us to know that some of the money we send to the Toomers will be used to keep his plane in the air.

How did it help us to go? Beyond feeling that we had made a difference with the work we did, we came away reminded once again of how blessed we are! It is so easy to enjoy our way of life back home and forget that thousands of people are dying every day for lack of clean water, food, and medicine. We forget that 40 percent of the people in the world today do not enjoy the use of electricity. If our power is off for 30 minutes, we get upset!

People who go on mission work teams do enjoy some sight-seeing. But what we see while in places like Ecuador usually changes our perspective about a lot of things. We become more grateful for what we have, and we begin to want to do something before we die to help the millions of people who have so little.

The face, the plight, and the need, of one little boy or girl in a remote jungle village can stay implanted in your mind for the rest of your life. That may be the most important result of going on a mission work team to a distant place like Shell. I am sure I will never be the same. +

A country preacher in Quito

𝕏

Sunday morning in Quito, the capital city of Ecuador, in faraway South America! By then we will have spent a whole day and two nights in this fine city, having flown out of Atlanta, with a brief stop in Houston, this past Friday. So what is a country preacher, an old one at that, doing way down here?

Actually Quito is not our final destination. We expect to travel by bus today to Shell, where we will work on a construction project for five days. Then we will make our way back home by returning the same route.

Shell is the base of operations for a group of missionaries on assignment with an organization known as MAF, or Missionary Aviation Fellowship. MAF is a global operation with bases all over the world. As the name implies, the main business of MAF is to help people in need through the use of airplanes, pilots, mechanics, and other service personnel.

Our connection with MAF's work in Shell is Sandy Toomer, a pilot. He and his wife, Trish, and their children have lived there for several years since choosing to become a missionary family. Our church family is one of the biggest supporters of the Toomers, who must raise all their support from churches and individuals.

So what will we be doing? We expect to continue the work others have begun in constructing another room for the base's school. Most projects are a joint effort with other mission work teams; one team takes up where another team leaves off. Another team from our church, 21 persons including several college students, worked at Shell for a week last month.

Our team will be the third team Trinity has sent to Shell. I am eager to find out why everyone who goes down there comes back ready to return. Dr. Joe Spano, of the Auburn Vet School, was on last month's team, along with his three sons. He said to me, "Pastor, you cannot imagine what a great time you will have down there!"

This will be my second trip to South America. My wife and I flew down to Brazil in 1996 when our church sent us to attend the World Methodist Conference. The worst part of such a trip is the long flight there. With knees like mine it is difficult to sit still for several hours. After four or five hours I am begging for mercy, and asking that anxious question my children used to ask a hundred times on a long trip, "Are we there yet?"

Where is Ecuador? It is south of Colombia, fronts on the Pacific Ocean, with Peru to the east and south. It is about the size of the state of Nevada with a population of 13 million people, mostly Indian and Spanish. The religion is mostly Roman Catholic.

Ask what the country produces and the answer, to no one's surprise, is bananas, coffee, cocoa, tapioca, sugarcane, cattle, balsa wood, etc. The main things exported are bananas, shrimp, fish, petroleum, and cut flowers. It was a surprise to me to learn that most of the roses sold in the United States come from Ecuador. Down there a dozen can be purchased for less than a dollar!

My preacher buddy, Jimmy Allen, brought back three dozen red roses to his wife, Anita. After learning that he spent less than three dollars for them, I imagine she asked, "What else did you bring me?" Ask Claude Brown why a dozen roses cost so much in Opelika and he would probably tell us that the shipping charges are unbelievable. Or perhaps he would have a speech about "whatever the traffic will bear."

Though I expect this to be a marvelous trip, I have an idea that, like everyone else, I will come back saying to my dear wife, "There really is no place like home!" +

People who need people

There is a popular song which has this memorable phrase in it: "People who need people are the luckiest people in the world." There is a lot of truth in that sentence.

Actually all people need people. But some people pretend not to need others. They can walk past you with a nod and a cheery word and you realize they did not need you - at least at that moment. We can give them a break and suppose that they were in a big hurry to do something important. Perhaps there was a good reason why they did not give you the time of day. There is no need to get on your high horse and criticize them. We are all guilty of brushing past people when we have something else on our mind. So there is no need for the pot to call the kettle black.

Then I suppose there are some people who, having taken offense at something we said or did, choose to ignore us intentionally. It is their way of saying, "You are no longer worthy of my respect and attention, you sorry so and so; now stay out of my life!" That can happen without our even knowing why the other party is offended. Such behavior causes most of us to become defensive. We are not guilty. They simply misunderstood what we said or did. That makes the break in our relationship their fault, not ours.

In this defensive stance we can take the attitude, "If you don't want to be friends with me, then fine. I can get along well without you too." That is the way some friendships come to an end. But sometimes friendships can be saved if one party is willing to eat a little humble pie and say to the other, "I regret what has happened between us and I want to apologize for whatever I may have done to offend you. Your friendship is important to me, and I want very much for us to become good friends again."

That attitude, however, is not possible in a person who feels no genuine need of people. Such a person actually needs other people but, having been hurt many times, refuses to admit the need of anyone else. In that frame of mind one may become quite caustic and bitter, and apologies are strongly repressed. The person who is hurt is apt to feel that it is the other person who owes him an apology.

Go back to the phrase in the song: "the luckiest people in the world." I know what the songwriter meant, but healthy friendships are actually not the result of "luck." The word "fortunate" says it much better. An even better choice might be "blessed." So we come nearer the truth when we say, "People who need people are the most fortunate (or blessed) people in the world."

The key is to understand our need of others and to be willing to admit it. Why is it so hard for some of us to admit we need people? Pride, I suppose, and our stubborn reluctance to let others know that we need their acceptance, friendship, and love.

A richer, healthier life is available to us when we are willing to swallow our silly pride and let other people know we need them. The truth is, people, all people, need people, and the sooner we freely admit it, the sooner life is worth living.

So, risk it. Pick out a person who seems to ignore you. If that is a person whose friendship you feel a need for, walk up and say, "I would like for us to be friends. If you have time for a cup of coffee, I'm buying. What do you say?"

"But what if I am rebuffed?" you ask. Look at it this way: to be rejected by another person will not diminish your worth one molecule! And there is no shame in offering your valuable friendship to another person. On the other hand, your admission of need might break the ice and allow a healthy friendship to develop. It's worth a try since we only go around once. Go for it! There is a good chance you will be blessed.
+

Things we should remember to forget

A man visiting his aged parents was impressed with the tender way his father addressed his mother. Whenever he spoke to her, or responded to her comments to him, he always used words like "baby," "honey," "sweetheart," or "darling." The son thought this was wonderful, that after more than 50 years of marriage, his father spoke so tenderly to his mother.

After awhile, when his mother was not in the room, the son complimented his father for using such lovely terms of endearment. A bit embarrassed, the old man replied, "Son, I have to use those pet names because for the past two months I have not been able to remember her name."

The loss of memory is actually not funny, though we may laugh about it and kid each other when it happens. Sometimes it can be quite tragic. Our friend Tom began slowly to lose his memory. One night his wife crawled into bed beside him, as it had been their custom for more than 40 years of marriage. He looked at her and said, "Who the devil are you?" Shocked, she replied, "I am your wife of course." To which he responded, "I don't know you; get out of my bed!" Their relationship went downhill after that as the man lost all awareness of his identity. He died without regaining it.

During the years of our lives most of us have the wonderful capacity to remember, and the equally wonderful capacity to forget. To live well there are things we must remember in order to be successful. But there are also things we must remember to forget if there is to be peace in our valley.

We must learn to forget the pain that occurred when someone hurt our feelings. To live is to be hurt from time to time, and often by those who love us, so we must be willing to forget those occasions and move on with our lives.

Unless we forget such pain we will soon harbor resentment, which can turn so easily into bitterness. Someone expressed this danger with this poignant comment: "Resentment is like taking poison and waiting for the other person to die." Simply put, resentment can kill you.

When Abraham Lincoln was discussing certain men he wished to promote during his presidency, an aide reminded him that one of the men had been especially critical of Lincoln. Asked if he had forgotten the man's criticism, Lincoln replied: "I remember deciding to forget about what he said." Because Lincoln could forget the man's faultfinding, he was able to recognize the man's gifts and recommend him for service. He refused to allow himself to be blinded by pain or resentment.

If we are unwilling to forget the slights and insults of others, we may allow ourselves to embrace anger, another attitude closely associated with resentment. Anger is another killer of the human spirit.

Recently the American Heart Association released the results of an exhaustive study on anger. This research involved monitoring 13,000 adults for six years. One of the key findings of this research is that a person with a propensity for anger is nearly three times more likely to have a heart attack than calmer persons. This ratio remained true even after researchers took into account other major risk factors such as smoking, obesity, and high blood pressure.

Other research at Duke University, led by psychiatrist Redford Williams, reveals that 20% of American adults have a susceptibility to anger high enough to threaten their health. So it is clear that our physical health can be positively affected by our willingness to forget the offensive behavior that produces anger in ourselves.

It behooves us, then, to take a good, honest look inside our memory. Are there things tucked away there that we should throw out? Are we holding on to hurts that happened years ago? Are these things ruining our health by producing unhealthy anger and resentment?

Every week some wonderful guys come by our homes driving what we call garbage trucks. Perhaps there are some painful memories we should let them pick up this week and haul away, out of our lives. If we are wise, there are indeed some things we must remember to forget. Only then can we make true what Robert Browning said, "The best is yet to be!" +

Advice for a grandson beginning college

※

Our grandson Joseph Albritton is 18 now and leaving home for college this month. He has enrolled in Pensacola Junior College and plans to live with his other grandparents in that coastal city.

So what advice can I give him as he begins this journey? A better question might be: Should I offer him any advice at all? I don't recall my parents giving me much counsel. I remember my mother stood in the yard crying as I drove away. My dad, a man of few words, simply said, "Do your best, son." Perhaps that was enough.

However, since I am not a man of few words, I am constrained to say more – and to give it in writing. So bear with me and try to decide if my advice has merit.

First, I must be honest and tell Joseph not to follow my example. I wasted my first year at Auburn. My study habits were poor. I majored in fun while enjoying the freedom of being away from parental discipline. By the end of the spring quarter I was in deep trouble. The Dean informed me that I would have to go to summer school and make A's and B's in order to remain a student in the fall.

Then I was introduced to something called "guidance counseling." That turned into a major blessing. Under the wise direction of a caring counselor, my life was turned around. Study became a daily routine – in the quietness of the old library on campus. I found out I could make good grades when I applied myself. That discovery motivated me to do well until I graduated.

So I will advise Joseph to apply himself diligently from the beginning so his first year will not be wasted.

Second, I will urge Joseph to resist the temptation to discard what he was taught in Sunday school and church. In college he will encounter some agnostics, and an occasional atheist, who will ridicule his Christian faith. He will hear more than he ever dreamed about the other major religions of the world. He will be invited to admit that Christianity is merely one religion among many, and that its claim for the divinity of Christ is obviously false.

He will be wise to listen and take such talk with a grain of salt. Listen and learn but hold on to biblical faith. When all the smoke clears, the Bible will still be the greatest book ever written. It will still contain God's truth. And those who deny God's truth cannot live well in a world created by God. God's word will remain true no matter how many academic degrees one may acquire.

Colleges should stretch our minds and enlarge our thinking. That is good. And agnostics and atheists get more attention than they deserve. I believe God has his witnesses on every campus. We should look for those teachers who will encourage us in the faith because they themselves are faithful disciples of Christ.

Even in seminary I had one professor who derided the Bible. His views were so bizarre that he was even tried for heresy, though not convicted. I learned from him but he was not a cherished mentor.

Finally, I will encourage Joseph to make up his mind soon about what he wants to do with his life. God has a plan for his life and only God can tell Joseph his true identity – the person he is meant to be. The sooner he discovers that, the sooner he can apply himself toward that goal.

When trains were young, the railroad company published a guide for travelers. It stated that before going on a journey the traveler should decide three things: 1) where he is going; 2) what train to take and when; and 3) whether he will have to change trains and where.

William Barclay calls this the best advice you could give a young person beginning the journey of life. He went on to say, "Anyone setting out on the journey of life ought to make up his mind clearly, firmly and early where he is going. He may not get there, but he will at least be trying to get somewhere. The person who does not know where he is going will literally get nowhere fast."

Young people like Joseph have to decide if they want to get all they can for themselves or if they want to do all they can for others. Do they want a job for the money or for the fulfillment the job can give? Dean Inge sums it up well: "The bored people are those who are consuming much but producing little."

One postscript: Joseph, don't forget the way home! Enjoy your new wings but remember your roots are here and there are people here in your balcony cheering for you to do your best! +

Chief Justice gets it right

Significant it is that the Chief Justice of the Alabama Supreme Court has offered us a book about character. I welcome the book but even more the idea that a prominent figure in the justice system would come forth with a stimulating defense of moral integrity.

I have not met Drayton Nabers, Jr. though I plan to seek him out. I want to meet him at least long enough to thank him for his new book, **The Case for Character**. A mutual friend, Randy Helms, gave me an autographed copy of the book for Christmas. Reading it has both inspired and encouraged me.

The Chief Justice has no qualms about using the Bible as his basic source of truth. Indeed, he boldly approaches character from a biblical perspective. This is refreshing in a culture that frowns at the very mention of words like God, Church, and Bible. The current exposure of the shameful greed of corporate business shows us what happens when a nation ignores God and biblical principles of living. This trend will only worsen unless men and women like Nabers can persuade us to reexamine the core values by which we live.

Nabers calls for his readers to help "recenter the character ethic in American life, in our churches, in our families, in our schools, and in ourselves." His recurring theme is that "we cannot be free spiritually, politically, morally, or economically without strong character." I found myself frequently offering an "Amen!" to his arguments.

I particularly enjoyed his chapter on love which he described as "seeking the best for others." My fondness for this chapter may have been influenced by the fact that years ago I too had been deeply moved by the heroic story of Robertson McQuilkin. What true character this man portrayed to us all!

McQuilkin was president of a college and seminary in South Carolina when his wife, Muriel, began showing signs of Alzheimer's disease. For several years he was able to balance his work and the care of his wife. However the time came when he resigned his presidency to devote his full time to the needs of his wife.

Nabers shares McQuilkin's moving letter of resignation:

"My dear wife, Muriel, has been in failing health for about 12 years. So far I have been able to carry both her ever-growing needs and my leadership responsibility at Columbia. But recently it has become apparent that Muriel is contented most of the time she is with me and almost none of the time I am away from her. It is not just 'discontent.' She is filled with fear – even terror – that she has lost me and always goes in search of me when I leave home. So it is clear to me that she needs me now, full-time.

"The decision was made, in a way, 42 years ago when I promised to care for Muriel 'in sickness and in health. . . till death do us part.' So, as a man of my word, integrity has something to do with it. But so does fairness. She has cared for me fully and sacrificially all these years; if I cared for her for the next 40 years I would not be out of her debt.

"Duty, however, can be grim and stoic. But there is more: I love Muriel. She is a delight to me – her childlike dependence and confidence in me, her warm love, and occasional flashes of wit I used to relish so, her happy spirit and tough resilience in the face of her continual depressing frustration. I don't have to care for her. I get to! It is a high honor to care for so wonderful a person."

Nabers slams home the point that love is much more than sentiment! As he says in his own words, "Like the abundant fruit of a healthy tree, love is the crowning glory of a character that allows us to glorify God and enjoy Him forever." Love, for Nabers, is the main thing. Get that right, he says, and you get everything else right. And he is right!

There are many other inspiring stories in the book, shared to highlight our need to value and develop strong character that honors God. I have shared the McQuilkin story to whet your appetite. I hope this tasty morsel will inspire you to get this book and read it. It deserves a wide audience in a decadent culture desperately in need of moral fiber. +

People of strong character inspire us

Why do we enjoy good books and stories of heroic people? Surely it is because such stories inspire us to live better lives ourselves. The stories of men and women of noble character motivate us to raise the bar of our own standards of living.

As I read through **The Case for Character** recently, I found myself looking for stories of exemplary people who have modeled strong character for us all. The author, Drayton Nabers, Jr., does not disappoint. The Chief Justice of the Alabama Supreme Court tells of many persons who help illustrate his case for the noble virtue of character.

The stories I like most are those that cause me to wonder if, in the same tough circumstances, I might have proven worthy of praise. We all like to think that, when the chips are down, we will not cave in to greed or self-interest but will do the right thing.

Nabers' story of a hotel manager is a good one to ponder. Would I have had courage like that of Paul Rusesabagina? Would you? Since I have no idea how to pronounce his last name, I will just call him Paul.

In 1994 Paul was manager of Rwanda's finest hotel. (You may have seen his story in the movie Hotel Rwanda.) That year the majority Hutu tribe began a ruthless campaign of genocide against the smaller Tutsi people. Paul was caught in the middle. He was a Hutu married to a Tutsi woman.

At first Paul offered refuge in his hotel only to family and friends. As the killing escalated, Paul risked his own life by taking in strangers. Soon his hotel housed over a thousand frightened people, mostly Tutsis. When the conflict finally ended, almost a million people had been killed. Somehow, though, Paul had managed to save the lives of almost all the people who had come to his hotel for safety.

What courage Paul demonstrated! Though his own life was in jeopardy, he put other people ahead of his own self-interest. Would you or I have had that kind of backbone? We like to think we would have had we been in his place. That is what attracts us to stories of courageous people.

Nabers reminds us of the power of example. He quotes Edmund Burke who said, "Example is the school of mankind. It will learn at no other." When I read that I remembered what Albert Schweitzer said: "There is one way and only one way to influence others, and that is by example."

The Chief Justice paid a beautiful tribute to his mother and the power of her example. He describes her as a humble, faithful, praying woman, full of patient hope, who modeled in her life the two keys to virtue – self-denial and perseverance.

His mother read to him and his two sisters every night. She enlisted his dad to read to the children also. The result of this reading is not surprising. Drayton observes, "We heard stories about virtuous people from the Bible and from classic children's stories and fables. These, too, modeled and engendered a desire for a morally good life."

You no doubt know that Albert Schweitzer was the most famous Christian missionary of the 20th Century. Would you suppose he was influenced by the character and example of his parents? If you think so, you are right. On Sunday afternoons young Albert's devout parents sat with him on the front porch and read stories of missionaries to the lad!

Winston Churchill was a man recognized for his strong character. He lived 90 years as a man who influenced nations by his example and decisions. I had no idea that Sir Winston was a man of such strong Christian principles until I read a book on his life written by Stephen Mansfield. It is a fine book titled ***The Character and Greatness of Winston Churchill***.

Mansfield tells of the influence not so much of Winston's parents but of his nanny – Elizabeth Everest. Churchill said he loved his mother "at a distance," but he adored Mrs. Everest. She taught him the Scriptures. She taught him to pray. She taught him to trust God. In times of trouble, he found himself praying prayers he had learned at his nanny's knee. No wonder that throughout his life a picture of Mrs. Everest sat on his desk and lay at his bedside when he died.

Can the character and examples of others influence our lives? You betcha! Little wonder then that we treasure the stories of noble people. Such stories can make a powerful, lasting difference in our lives. +

The Lone Ranger's Safety Club

Ж

I am old enough to remember when the mail was delivered by the mail man. I remember him being a kind man and old. Mama would buy postage stamps from him. He never seemed in a hurry but always brought the mail about the same time every day.

Nowadays the mail man may be a woman. Our mail carrier lately has been an attractive young woman. For the first time in years I have wished you could still buy stamps from the mail man. My wife says I should buy them at the Post Office in town.

As a child I seldom got mail except on my birthday when I received a few cards from Mama's sisters. I remember how special it was to receive a card or a letter with my name on it. At Christmas, with Mama's encouragement, I would write a letter to Santa Claus but he never wrote me back.

One day I got a letter from the Lone Ranger. My excitement was deflated when I opened the envelope. It was not from the Lone Ranger after all, but from his staff. I had been accepted as a member of the Lone Ranger Safety Club. Enclosed was a nice certificate of membership, with my name on it.

That certificate was special. I hung it on the wall beside my bed. It made me feel that I was somebody. I can still remember how proud I felt. I was not just a poor country boy out in the woods. The Lone Ranger knew me and I belonged to his club.

That has been a long time ago, but I know now that it was the Lone Ranger who got me into the mess I am in. He sold his address list to some friends and ever since then I have been getting tons of mail from people wanting me to join their clubs.

I was impressed at first. Superman wanted me to join his club, and for seven dollars I could learn all about kryptonite and how Superman got to the earth. But seven bucks was a fortune back then so I had to be content with my Lone Ranger membership.

As the years went by I realized it was impossible to belong to every club that wanted to include me. But by the time I got smart enough to know what was happening I had joined a book club and a record club. My wife and I had to build a shed to house all our books and long-playing records. Somewhere in our piles of stuff we still have some of Johnny Cash's first records though the string music of Mantivani's orchestra was our favorite.

Being pack rats my wife and I have difficulty throwing anything away. So we still find room in the house for some of those books that the club thought we should read. I wasted several hours trying to read Napoleon's memoirs but finally gave up. Since he was a general he should have hired a ghost writer like the presidents do.

Back in February I attended a seminar on woodworking. Since then my mailbox has been loaded with invitations to join woodwork book clubs and subscribe to at least four woodworking magazines. It never ends.

Once I was a lonely, unknown country boy longing to be known and have significance as a person. Now a thousand organizations are sending me mail, clamoring for my money and offering me membership in their clubs. We may have to get a second trash can just for the junk mail.

How my life has changed. Once I longed to get a letter with my name on it. Now I write two or three letters every week asking various "clubs" and organizations to remove my name from their mailing list.

I never thought it would come down to this but I have to admit it – I have a grudge against the Lone Ranger. If he had not sold that mailing list I might not be drowning in this raging sea of junk mail. +

Handling grief difficult for children

X

Every Thursday I carve out some time to write something for the Sunday paper. This Thursday morning my grandson Jake Albritton is attending a funeral. It is a rare experience for a 14-year-old.

The deceased was a mentor and schoolmate of Jake's. Bryan Valliere, 18, was killed last Sunday in a one-vehicle accident on US Highway 231 in Wetumpka. A friend and younger classmate was driving the truck.

From all accounts Bryan was an exceptional young man. An excellent student, good athlete, devout Christian, and Eagle Scout, Bryan was scheduled to graduate in May. Jake got to know Bryan at Edgewood Academy where both played on the football team.

School was cancelled so students could attend Bryan's funeral at Thelma Baptist Church near Wetumpka. The entire school was mourning the loss of one of its finest students.

Bryan took a special interest in our grandson. Jake had a rare opportunity as an eighth grader to practice football with the seniors. Edgewood is a small school and Coach Bobby Carr wanted the younger boys to bond with the older ones. A lineman himself, Bryan saw potential in Jake and encouraged him. Jake looked up to Bryan and admired him as a role model and good friend.

I will not attend the funeral but I will be praying for Jake and his classmates. Their school lessons have been put aside this week. Basketball games have been cancelled. The focus of the school has shifted to one thing: the sudden, tragic death of a promising young man.

Death is like that. It will rear its ugly head and slap you in the face when you are least expecting it. Jake was in the woods hunting when a friend called on his cell phone to tell him about Bryan's death. Jake stood beside a tree and wept as the awful news shook him.

That is often the way we meet death. One day you are carefree, enjoying the good life. The next moment you are numb, shocked into disbelief by the abrupt ending of someone's life. It makes no sense. Questions beginning with the word "Why" jam the switchboard of your brain.

Jake's jarring encounter with death is reminiscent of my own introduction to the Grim Reaper when I was about Jake's age. My cousin "Buck" Johnson died ironically on the same highway, US 231, north of Montgomery. It was also a one-vehicle accident in a truck. Buck was only 13 when his life ended in much the same way that Bryan's did – in a ditch beside the highway.

Buck and I were good friends. We enjoyed playing together whenever our families shared a meal on holidays. Suddenly he was gone. No one could explain to me why he had to die. I found no answers that made any sense.

So I am praying for Jake. He will grow up a lot this week. His life will never be the same. Mine was not. There was a gripping new awareness of the reality of death, a sobering realization that young people might not live to be old just because they wished it so.

There is another coincidence in Jake's experience and my own. Seniors write out a "Last Will and Testament" that is printed in most high school annuals. Bryan had already written his. A teacher called Jake aside and told him that Bryan had included him in his last will. He had "willed" his football jersey number, 79, to Jake.

I imagine Jake will wear 79 for the rest of the time he plays football. He will never forget his friend Bryan or the special gift he left him. Even more, I have an idea that Jake's memory of Bryan's influence will motivate him to become a good role model for other young men. He will want to continue the legacy left to him by this splendid fellow student.

I wish I had saved my Wetumpka High football jersey. It would be old and tattered but if I had it, I would give it to Jake to hang on his wall. My number was also 79.

Today, with Jake, I share the grief of Bryan's family and pray for all who mourn the loss of this outstanding young man. My heart is heavy for them all, but especially for the children.

Coping with grief is so difficult for children. Hopefully those of us who are older and a little wiser can provide the love, hope, and understanding that children need in such an hour. +

Keeping Christmas a wonderful idea

Christmas is over. We ate too much. We have thrown away the wrapping paper, saved the bows, and cannot remember who gave us what. Now we turn to football games by the dozen and ponder resolutions for the New Year.

As we say goodbye to Christmas, I can think of nothing more beautiful to share with you than my favorite piece written by Henry van Dyke. Van Dyke was a Presbyterian pastor and later in life professor of English literature at Princeton University. He was born in Germantown, Pennsylvania, in 1852 and died in 1933.

Van Dyke was a gifted writer and published several books. You may recall reading some quotations credited to him. Here are two good ones:

"Use the talents you pos¬sess, for the woods would be ve¬ry sil¬ent if no birds sang ex¬cept the best."

"Time is too slow for those who wait, too swift for those who fear, too long for those who grieve, too short for those who re¬joice, but for those who love, time is eter¬ni¬ty."

But surely the best thing for which van Dyke is remembered is his marvelous essay on "Keeping Christmas." I hope you enjoy it as much as I do.

There is a better thing than the observance of Christmas Day,
and that is keeping Christmas.
Are you willing to forget what you have done for other people
and to remember what other people have done for you?
To ignore what the world owes you
and to think what you owe the world?
To see that your fellow men are just as real as you are?
To try to look behind their faces to their hearts,
hungry for joy?
To close your book of complaints
against the management of the universe
And look around you for a place where you can sow
a few seeds of happiness?

To admit that the only good reason for your existence is
not what you are going to get out of life,
but what you are going to give to life?
Are you willing to do these things, even for a day?
Then you can keep Christmas.
Are you willing to stoop down and consider the needs
and desires of little children?
To remember the weakness and loneliness
of people who are growing old?
To stop asking how much your friends like you?
and ask yourself whether you love them enough?
To trim your lamp so that it will give more light and less smoke,
And to carry it in front so your shadow will fall behind you?
To try to understand what those who live
in the same house with you really want,
without waiting for them to tell you?
To make a grave for your ugly thoughts
and a garden for your kindly feelings?
Are you willing to do these things even for a day?
Then you can keep Christmas.
Are you willing to believe that love
is the strongest thing in the world --
stronger than hate, stronger than death --
and that the blessed life which began in
Bethlehem nineteen hundred years ago is the image
and brightness of eternal love?
Then you can keep Christmas.
But you can never keep it alone.

+

What is Right about Christmas

I am weary of the complaints some Christians are always making about the commercialization of Christmas. The kingdom of God is not advanced by focusing on what is wrong. So let's call time out and celebrate what is right about Christmas.

There is nothing wrong with buying and selling gifts. If we spend more than we can afford, that is wrong. Going in debt to buy stuff is not good. But sharing gifts with loved ones and friends is a good thing. Christmas motivates people to give. For a few weeks most of us are less selfish than at any other time of the year. That's good.

There is nothing wrong about making children happy. Children love Christmas. The anticipation of a nice gift under the tree stimulates the mind and the spirit. To open a gift given by someone who loves you makes you glad to be alive. That's good.

The stores sell more stuff in December than any other month of the year. So business owners are happy. I see nothing wrong with business making a profit on the sale of goods. Christmas stimulates economic growth. That should make us all happy. If, of course, we go in debt buying more than we can afford, then we exchange our happiness for the pain of excessive debt. The secret is to spend wisely, not extravagantly.

Some holy souls think Santa Claus should be banned from Christmas. It is, after all, the birth of Jesus, not pagan old Santa. Well, wait a minute. Santa Claus was important to me before I met Jesus. I loved the old fellow and I still do. He was good to me as a child. Santa made Christmas fun by coming down that chimney and leaving gifts that made my eyes dance with delight on Christmas morning.

We don't have to kick Santa out to honor Jesus at Christmas. Untold millions of children receive gifts at Christmas because people feel compelled to "be Santa" to neglected children. In a strange way Santa and Jesus seem to be partners in stirring people to help others at Christmastime. That is not bad.

Children like to go caroling at Christmas. They don't go to nursing homes and sing carols in May or August. They do love to do it at Christmas. And lonely seniors at nursing homes will tell you they love to have them come sing carols for them. That's a fine thing about Christmas.

Christmas is a time for parties. We have been to several parties and enjoyed them all. Parties are fine. You can enjoy fellowship and good food with friends in a lovely setting. That's good. If you eat too much or get drunk at these parties, that's bad. Even Santa would tell you that (not to mention Jesus).

Instead of complaining about commercialization, pastors should admit they love Christmas. People give more generously in December than any other month of the year. Without the offerings received in December most churches would never meet their budgets. Believe me, that's good.

People love to come home for Christmas. That's better than good; that is wonderful. When we lived out of state for several years, we always made our way home for Christmas. Now that we are old, our hearts are filled with joy when our children and grandchildren come home for Christmas. That is actually one of the best gifts of Christmas – to have our family home to share a meal, exchange gifts, and love on one another.

Of course Christmas is about a baby named Jesus who was born to save us from our sins. Christmas is about grace and grace is about giving. God gave. He gave us his Son. That gift motivates us to give – and to love. Yes, this is what we preachers call the deeper meaning of Christmas. But we don't have to become so spiritual that we spoil Christmas for the children.

Commercialization should not prevent us from celebrating the spiritual reality of Christmas. Santa Claus is no threat to the Savior of the world. Jesus is so much bigger than Santa that I can imagine Jesus saying, "Santa, come sit on my knee and let me thank you for all the joy you have brought to children for centuries." Can't you see the smile that would bring to the face of Jolly Old Saint Nicholas?

Hey, loosen up guys. Let's relax and enjoy what is right about Christmas. +

A Christmas Letter to My Wife

My Dearest Dean,

Christmas means more to me this year than ever before. I hope I get to sit down with you in front of a nice fire, sip some hot apple cider together, and tell you why. But in case that occasion eludes us, you may have to settle for reading my thoughts in print.

When you were struggling to breathe a few days ago, and we were making a mad dash to the emergency room, I thought I might lose you. Your breathing was so shallow. It hurt me so to see you struggling to breathe.

Yet I saw no panic in your eyes. That seemed impossible at the time though you told me later than you were "at peace" about dying. I was touched to hear you say later that you felt no fear of dying if the Lord had decided to call you home. You said you felt your life was in God's hands.

Of course dying is not a new subject for us. You and I have talked about death many times, realizing that death is a natural part of life. The death of our little boy made us keenly aware, as young parents, that life may have an abrupt ending at any point on the journey. I have felt for many years that David's death in some way lessened our own fear of dying.

I hope that somehow I can be as calm as you were in the face of my own death. Though I am not eager to die, I sense a certain readiness in my own heart to step across the threshold into the hands of Jesus. I pray that I am ready to meet our Lord. Thank God we both know that salvation depends not on our merit but upon the mercy of the loving Father we have trusted since we were children.

What makes this Christmas mean so much more is our awareness of the wonderful ways God has been at work in our lives. Fifty-eight years of marriage gives us a rather long view of things. When we look backward we see God at work repeatedly. He was in every mess we made. Now we know that it was his grace that made the difference.

The first summer of our marriage we kept a Persian cat for a neighbor while she traveled to Europe. Remember? She gave us a dollar a day to keep that cat and for two months we swallowed cat hairs until I was ready to scream. That was the hardest money we ever earned. But God was there and we made it.

When our boy was struggling with leukemia, we played the LP record of "Jesu, Joy of Man's Desiring" night after night. Only God could have put that music in our little rented house. We knew so little of the significance of Bach's music back then. Yet unknowingly we drank the "joy of deathless springs" during those bewildering nights, waiting for Jesu to take our boy home. But God was there and we made it.

There were those times when our marriage was coming apart at the seams. My career seemed to mean more to me than my family. You got tired of being Dad and Mom to four boys without receiving much help from me. Only God kept you from killing me. But once again God was there and somehow we made it.

Then finally we were grandparents and more recently great grandparents. We thought we had problems raising four sons. But God has shown us what real problems are as we have watched our grandchildren struggle with the demons of this world.

We made more than our share of mistakes raising our boys but God was there and we made it. What is more wonderful is that the boys made it. They survived their own struggles and chose finally to trust our Jesu.

In trying to persuade our grandchildren to embrace Jesu we have made even more mistakes. We have been slow to let God have his way with our children and grandchildren. Often we have tried to fix things ourselves and found we were wrong. But through it all, God was there and we made it.

As we see the shadows lengthening we realize that, like everybody else, our days are numbered. We too will slip away some morning or some evening and find ourselves on the other shore. But until God wills our departure I plan to celebrate every waking moment and to seize the joy of each new day. More than ever I find myself listening to you breathe while you are sleeping and I thank God for you. I thank him for the great gift he has given me – having you by my side for so many years.

This Christmas means so much more to me because I still have you, and we have each other, and we have our precious family. I look back not with regret but with gratitude because I know now better than I have ever known it that God was there, in every mess, and because he was with us, we made it.

That convinces me that Jesu is real and because he is with us, we can make it all the way to the end. And the end after all is the beginning of all that awaits us on the other side. Until then, my prayer is that this will be the best Christmas we have ever shared.

Merry Christmas!

Your grateful husband,

Walter, sjc +

The passing of a friend

✕

They called it "a massive heart attack." One minute my friend John Knowles was alive; the next he was dead. The good Methodists at First Church buried John two days later. My friend Melinda Jackson told me that had a good funeral for John. His pastors spoke well of him.

Now he is gone and I miss him already. There will be no more long telephone calls listening to John share about the ups and downs of his unusual life. No more questions about whether he should return to Russia. No more talks about the demons he fought, or about the extent of God's mercy.

The time I first saw John is etched in my mind. He came forward as we were singing the last hymn in a Sunday morning worship service in Opelika. He had been deeply moved by the Spirit of God not merely to join the church but to get right with God.

John and I met together frequently after that. We became good friends partly because he and I fought some of the same demons. We could identify with each other. We had walked some of the same trails, and had shared some of the same trials.

John's temper got the best of him sometimes. I understood that. Mine has dogged me most of my life. I liked John's transparency. He was many things but he was not the Great Pretender. He told me the truth about the dark side of his life and I shared mine with him.

John knew the deep pain of shame. When things had not gone right, John was embarrassed, enough to sense his need of God's mercy. I remember especially one day John walked into my study, closed the door, and said in a sober tone, "When I walk out that door, I want to know that God has forgiven me of all my sins, so we have got to do some serious praying."

We did not sit and talk very long. Soon we were on our knees talking to the Lord, pleading for mercy, not just for John but for me as well. I never help anyone seek mercy without asking for some myself. I guess that is one reason John trusted me. He knew I was not a holy, righteous preacher asking God to help a vile sinner. When John and I prayed, we were two men in need, praying side by side and believing that God wanted to make us both clean and holy in his sight.

Like all men, John fell from grace a time or two. (If dear reader, you think you have never fallen, then don't look now but the demon Pride has you by the nap of the neck.) The good news is that John knew the way back home. He was sure that God would forgive a repentant sinner. Repeatedly John escaped from Satan's snares and found peace again with God.

I remember another time John met me at the altar. He was convinced that God wanted him to go to Russia and do missionary work. Though I was reluctant to send him, John insisted on going. He served there for a time, came home for rest and renewal, and went back. His life there was not easy in Russia, but he endured it in obedience to God.

Like the best of us, John had his shortcomings. We disagreed about many issues. A few times I chastised John until tears were on both our cheeks. But he had a heart for God. He loved God. He wanted to serve God. He loved Cynthia, and his children Drue and Blair. He loved his church in Lanett, even when for an interval he belonged to Trinity in Opelika. John felt a deep gratitude for the mercy of God. He was my friend. I will miss those long conversations on the telephone.

Life can end so abruptly. Our days here are indeed like a vapor or a shadow. We are here for a little while and then we are gone. The sudden passing of a good friend reminds us of the brevity of life. Often this reminder can be a wake-up call to put things in order and prepare for our own departure.

One thing is certain as I mull these sober thoughts. No matter how long or how short our days on earth, life is made richer by true friends. John Knowles was one of mine, and today I give thanks for his friendship. +

Caring for people makes a difference

※

A great lesson life has taught me is that people are blessed more by our caring than by our opinions. Yet many people seem oblivious to this truth.

If we are at all teachable most of us learn this basic truth in a hundred different ways. We learn it early as children. Wise parents do not insist that their children agree with them in all things; they recognize that people are different and even encourage individuality in their children.

Some children, for example, will not like spinach but may enjoy green beans. What is important is that children eat green vegetables, not that they are forced to eat spinach. Since green beans will do the trick, there is no need to blow a gasket because a child refuses to eat spinach.

The use of such wisdom by loving parents helps us to grasp this truth: Love is essential even though opinions may be different. So what matters is that a child feel loved, not that the child shares all the opinions of the parents.

My parents had strong feelings about many things. When I was growing up, they refused to work on Sundays unless the ox was in the ditch. They would not allow me or my siblings to go to a movie on Sunday. These and other principles they instilled in us when we were young. But they did not disown us when, as adults, we began to disagree with some of their opinions.

What I finally realized after many years as an adult is that my parents modeled this truth in our home for their children – caring is vastly more important than opinions. Opinions are really a dime a dozen. Love, however, is a fundamental need of the human spirit. Without genuine caring, all the opinions in the world are worthless.

I learned this concept also as a pastor. People are not sitting in their homes waiting for the pastor to come by and share his opinions about everything under the sun. Actually this is so true that nobody really gives a hoot about what the pastor thinks – until they know he has a heart, and that he truly cares about people.

This has given birth to the dictum that most pastors have embraced:

people do not care what you know until they know that you care. Some pastors have learned the hard way that people will not even listen to their opinions, much less really hear them, until they know deep down that their pastor cares about them.

As a brash young pastor I had opinions about everything – from the evil of drinking alcohol to the phony healing services of television evangelist Oral Roberts. I learned fairly quickly that people were not waiting with baited breath to hear what I thought; they were wondering if I had any compassion to share with them.

The real bore for me today is the person who pretends to know something about every subject and is chomping at the bit to spray the air with his inflexible views. You can never have a decent conversation with that person; all you can do is listen or walk away.

Everywhere you turn in our culture you are bombarded with opinions – about healthcare, the oil spill, cloning, Iraq, abortion, the President, illegal immigrants, medicine, fraud, crime, the warming of the earth, and a thousand other things. There are so many opinions you hardly know whose you can trust.

The bottom line for me is simply this: Opinions become useful only within the context of love, and nobody wants to know what you think until they know you care about them. Are we not all fed up with opinions – but still hungry for love?

Care about me and I may listen to your opinions but please, keep them to yourself until I ask you what you think. And do remember to shut up real often – so you can hear what I think.

There is a good chance we may disagree, but that will be alright as long as I know you care about me and you know that I care about you.
+

Valuable lessons from Robert E. Lee

☒

My son Tim, an experienced forester, is an admirer of Robert E. Lee. When he learned how much I liked the new book on character by Alabama Chief Justice Drayton Nabers Jr., he suggested we swap books.

He wanted me to read one of his favorite books – ***Robert E. Lee On Leadership*** by H. W. Crocker III. I found it a delightful book, full of Lee's "secrets" for successful leaders and fascinating stories of his courageous leadership during the cruel war between the South and the North.

It has been fun to note the passages highlighted by Tim and to celebrate his desire to be a good leader and a man of exemplary character like his mentor Lee. Tim will never lead an army but he has become a man whose strength of character is worthy of imitation.

General Lee was known as "the Grey Fox." The blue-coated "hounds" of General Ulysses S. Grant failed repeatedly in their attempts to trap Lee. Though usually outnumbered two to one, Lee inspired his troops to stymie the Union Army throughout the war. Even though his men were tattered and hungry, their stinging assaults inflicted 50,000 casualties on the Federals in a single month – May, 1864.

Still, in the end the North's superiority led at last to Lee's surrender at Appomattox Court House. Crocker describes in his book the incredible cost of the war to General Lee:

"A successful soldier, he was not used to defeat. Now he had lost his home, his career, and virtually all his worldly goods – including his carefully harbored savings and investments. Worse, he had suffered the premature death of a daughter, a daughter-in-law, two grandchildren, and countless colleagues and friends.

"A patriot who had devoted his life to the service of his country, who venerated George Washington, who was the son of a Revolutionary War hero ('Light Horse Harry' Lee), and who had married Martha Washington's great-granddaughter, Lee was now deprived of his citizenship and liable to be tried for treason. His home state of Virginia was under occupation, its citizens deprived of their rights, its fields, towns, and cities devastated by the Union's policy of total war.

"And yet . . . and yet, Lee was not defeated. Soon after the war's end, he was increasingly regarded not merely as a military genius but as someone to be venerated by the South and by the North, to be venerated, indeed, throughout the Western world as a great man."

I hope this lengthy quote will whet your appetite enough that you will want to read this good book. Crocker generated my profound admiration for the man Winston Churchill called "one of the noblest Americans who ever lived, and one of the greatest captains known to the annals of war."

The author provides many examples to support his claim that Lee's greatness sprang not from what he did but from what he was, and the way he lived. Lee was not merely a military genius; he was a gentleman, so much so that even his enemies admired him.

Douglas Southall Freeman, who wrote a four-volume biography of General Lee, wrote this concluding remark, "I have been fully repaid by being privileged to live, as it were, for more than a decade in the company of a great gentleman."

One of Crocker's conclusions is worth noting: "In our own materialistic age, we can especially benefit from Lee's example of leadership, which reminds us that ultimately what matters is not how much money we have made, how many businesses we have led or acquired, how many jobs we have created, or how many 'toys' we have accumulated, but who we are."

Lee, Crocker observes, "is an ever-present reminder that we can be much more."

There are indeed many valuable lessons that Robert E. Lee can teach us about how to live a noble life! I commend Crocker's book to anyone wishing to live a truly successful life. +

Holding the hand of a good friend

)(

The man who called me made an unusual request. "Walter, I need a favor. Could you find a man who could come to my apartment in the morning and hold my hand for awhile?"

He went on to explain. The movers were coming to pack up his things so that the following day he could move into a nursing home nearby. "It is not easy," he said with feeling, to box up all my stuff and move again at age 83."

I assured him I could find a man to do what he wanted. So the next day I showed up. I was the man. I wanted to be that man. I would not have missed that chance for a million dollars.

Russ is a gracious man. His mind is still sharp. He is a bit unsteady on his feet but he can still move around on his own, albeit very slowly. I poured myself a cup of coffee and watched with him the men who carefully boxed his belongings.

He commented about the blank walls. The pictures were down and boxed up. "I will be able to hang some of them in my new quarters but not all of them. My place at the nursing home is much smaller so I will probably have to store some of my things." He seemed to feel alright about that.

We talked for awhile until my friend said, "Why don't we go have lunch together?" I told him I had hoped he would suggest doing that. We talked some more about the past as we shared "Po Boy" sandwiches at a nearby deli.

Russ told me about Evelyn, the dear wife he had lost some 14 years before. He has missed her. Life has not been the same though I sensed that he had made a heroic effort to carry on without his precious companion.

They lived in Atlanta for 41 years. Then, having moved into his eighties, he decided to move to Montgomery to be near his son's family. That chapter was over now. He was no longer able to take good care of himself. It was nursing home time.

He seemed surprisingly upbeat about living in the nursing home. "They serve excellent food there; I have sampled their cooking twice already."

At the nursing home he will not have to do his own cooking. He seemed pleased that he would have three meals a day prepared for him. He looks forward to that, even expecting that he might have to watch his weight.

"They have a beautiful dining room there," he said. "Have you seen it?" he asked me. I told him I had seen it one day when I gave a devotional to some of the residents. He said he hoped I would come and speak there again, and I assured him I would so I could visit with him.

Russ was pleased that I would take the time to sit with him and chat awhile. I assured him the privilege was mine. I explained it this way. I am only a few years behind him and I hope someone will come hold my hand when it comes my time to make such a move.

The dogwoods are beginning to bloom in our town. Trees are exploding with buds. It is beginning to look a lot like spring even in mid-March. But I don't think Russ paid much attention to nature's emerging beauty. He was wondering how it would be to unbox his stuff and start life over again in his new digs. Once again he would have to do it without his dear Evelyn by his side.

As you have probably guessed by now, I never held Russ' hand. That was simply a figure of speech. He simply wanted a friend to be with him as he bravely faced yet another of the challenges the aging must handle.

There were no tears, no sighs of regret, no complaining, and no self-pity. His words as we parted were positive and cheerful. "I will be alright," he said, and I know he will. He asked for no sympathy. I gave him none, only my deepest respect.

The movers came the next morning. Our mutual friend Ray Caudle dropped by like I did – to hold his hand and drive him to the nursing home.

How Ray feels I do not know. I know how I feel. I feel so blessed that this good friend honored me with the high privilege of holding his hand as he thanked God for what has been and welcomed with joy what is to come.

I wish the world had more men in it like Russ Krantz. +

Take time to visit a sick friend

Ⅺ

"Do you enjoy visiting the sick?" The question surprised me since it was posed by a friend who, like me, is a retired pastor. I needed little time to ponder my answer.

"Of course," I replied. "Visiting the sick gives me the opportunity to practice Christianity at its best – one on one."

My friend shook his head. He said, "During all my years in the ministry the thing I disliked the most was visiting the sick. And that is what I like about being retired – I don't have to make hospital and nursing home calls anymore."

Our conversation reminded me that we all have different gifts and strengths. We are all wired differently. What turns one person on may not turn his best friend on. I respect my friend; he respects me. I do not think I am right and he is wrong. We are simply different.

My present ministry involves visiting the sick. Some are sick at home. Some are in nursing homes. Others are physically impaired and for the most part homebound. Sometime most of us become hospital patients for a few days because of illness or the need for surgery.

I truly enjoy visiting sick persons for several reasons. The most important is that it gives me an opportunity to offer compassion to people at a time when it is most needed. We all have a basic need to be loved – and what better time to receive love from a caring friend than when you are anxious about your health.

Christianity is more than doctrine, more than ritual, more than worship and singing, more than programs and buildings; it is a relationship with Christ that motivates you to care about others. Without compassion, there is no genuine Christianity.

Compassion can be shared in other ways, of course, than visiting sick people. Such visitation is simply one concrete way of caring for others, and some of us find it an enjoyable ministry.

I like visiting the sick because it gives me a chance to cheer people up.

A cheerful spirit is almost always welcome in a hospital room. A sour spirit is never welcome nor does it help anyone. What most people need is someone who will encourage them, offer them hope for the future, and help them to feel better about themselves.

A cheerful word wrapped in a smile is good medicine for the soul. At my age I usually put my hand gently on the forehead of a sick person as I offer a prayer. Touching people with compassion will never go out of style. Jesus taught us that. We may not be able to heal people as he did but we can touch them with love knowing that love often becomes a channel of God's healing power.

I love visiting sick people in the hospital because of what it meant to me when I was desperately ill in the hospital myself. I don't remember what my friends said when they visited me; I just remember that they were there. Their presence made a difference that I cannot explain. My heart continues to be full of gratitude for the people who took the time to come by my hospital bed to let me know they cared about me.

Prolonged visits with the sick are not desirable. I understand that. A good visit need not be more than a few minutes. Loving concern can be conveyed in a few words with a warm smile and a brief prayer.

Jesus felt visiting the sick was very important. His words can be motivating when I am weary and my body is directing me toward my easy chair. He made it clear that how we respond to the needs of others will determine our final destiny.

He even put himself into the picture. If I fail to visit the least of my brothers when they are sick, I have failed to visit him. That is what he said. I don't think he wanted us to visit the sick for the wrong motive – out of fear that we would not go to heaven.

He wanted our chief motive to be love. He wanted us to care for others because we have compassion for them. He knew that if we would drop what we are doing and take the time to visit a friend in the hospital, we would be doing ourselves a favor. That is because ultimately we are the ones who are blessed the most by an act of kindness extended to another. +

Only one thing lasts forever

)|(

The most unusual gift ever given me is a piece of stone from the city of Split in Croatia. My dear friend Klaus Guenzel gave me the stone as a gracious expression of his friendship. Klaus is a lieutenant colonel in the German Air Force.

I pressed him to tell me the stone's history and why he gave it to me. His answer was as unusual as the stone itself and made the stone powerfully significant to me. So let me explain why it has become one of my most treasured possessions.

Klaus found the stone in ruins near what was once the beautiful palace built at the end of the third century by Roman Emperor Diocletian. The palace was situated on the Adriatic Coast in Split, now one of the largest cities in Croatia, formerly the Republic of Yugoslavia.

Was the stone once part of a proud palace column? Perhaps, though no one knows. It may have been and that is the point Klaus made to me. Imagine the power of the emperor. He could send thousands of soldiers to do his bidding. Rome ruled the world and Diocletian was its mighty ruler.

People stood in awe and fear of the great Roman Empire. They imagined it would last forever for no other nation on earth could match the power of Rome.

Now Rome is gone. Its mighty emperors strut their stuff no more. My piece of stone reminds me that empires come and go. Proud marble palaces eventually crumble and fall. Even my little stone will one day be little more than a handful of sand and dust.

Klaus asks me to tell him what does last. Does anything last forever? He answers his own question by quoting Jesus: "Heaven and earth will disappear, but my words will remain forever." My little stone reminds me that only one thing lasts forever – Jesus and his words. They will never lose their power. They will remain when all the world's palaces lie in ruins.

Honestly I had never heard of the city of Split, though I had heard about Emperor Diocletian. I have marveled this week at the message of my stone. I have thought of old Diocletian. Once he was the most powerful man on earth. Now he is but a footnote in the history books.

No one remembers a word he ever said.

Jesus, on the other hand, is quoted by millions of people. His words are so powerful they have been translated into almost every language in the world. His words remain, and so does he.

One simple sentence spoken by Jesus will be proclaimed with confident joy on this Day of Resurrection on every continent – "Because I live, you will live also!"

Today many will hear the story of the big stone that was rolled away from the tomb, but I will let my precious little stone speak to me its message of eternal hope. I will thank God for my brother Klaus whose gift of friendship is even more precious than the stone. And I will thank God for this most unusual gift that will always remind me of the one thing that lasts forever – the words of our Risen Lord.

Hallelujah! He lives! +

When it is time to take a walk

※

Thursday was a miserable day. It started with an early morning Bible study. The instructor kept talking about me. I could not wait to get out of there.

All he could talk about was patience. He began listing the ways most men are impatient. Normally I take notes but not Thursday. It would have looked like a confessional. Somebody might read it. I glanced at my watch. Good grief! I still had 45 minutes to endure.

Our leader seemed unusually cheerful as he ranted on and on. Why not? He was not confessing his own sins; no, none of that. He was too busy stepping on our toes, especially mine.

Men reveal their impatience when buying fast food, he said. We complain if it takes 10 minutes instead of five to receive our order. What is wrong with that? Fast food should be fast food. Who wants to waste gas for 10 minutes in a drive-thru line? There are things to do.

Then he attacked grocery shopping of all things. I had to admit he was right. When I turn the corner at the last aisle and head toward the check-out lines, I feel like a stallion at the Kentucky Derby. Seeing a short line, I race to beat a little old lady pushing a ton of groceries. I win, only to discover that in front of me is another old lady with two tons of groceries in her cart. The thrill of victory fades into the agony of defeat.

Male impatience is obvious on the highway. We risk accidents trying to keep another fellow from cutting in front of us. On the interstate some of us are control freaks; we want to control what lane other cars can use. I admit; I am guilty. I hate to move over for some nut driving 85 mph.

Guys are also impatient with their wives; he had to bring them up. He said, "You get home at dark, tired from a long day at work, and supper is not ready. The house is not cleaned. So you bark at your wife, demanding to know what on earth she has been doing."

Finally I was off the hook. My wife cook supper? You have got to be kidding. I can't remember when she cooked a meal. We always eat out. Doesn't everybody? I disconnected the stove in our kitchen back in '04 so the clock on it would not use so much electricity. New homes do not even have kitchen stoves these days, do they?

I was puzzled. Do women still do house cleaning? I thought they had given that up for Lent years ago. My wife's idea of house cleaning is to point me toward the vacuum cleaner. Why me? It is too heavy for her, she says. I finally bought a good one but it is heavy, so it is mine.

We used to wash dishes together, one of those fun things we enjoyed as a happily married couple. She washed and I dried. Now we have a dish washer. All the fun is gone and it takes twice as long to do the dishes. She washes them by hand and then puts them in the dish washer. I have to turn away; that is too much for me. Why wash the dishes twice? When she is not looking, I refuse to put the detergent in the dish washer. I can save a little that way since the dishes are already washed, but I hate using all that expensive hot water.

Suddenly guilt swept over me. I realized how really impatient I am with my wife – about the pillows on the bed and moving furniture. I started to sweat, hoping the men at my table would not notice. Why can't I relax about having 19 pillows piled on our bed? Why is a bed not made up until all those pretty pillows are arranged neatly at the head?

Years ago, back in '01 I think, I gave up arguing about the pillows. I get rid of my frustration by tossing the pillows, one at a time, on the other side of the room each night. I thought she would be proud of me for making fun out of a problem. That has not happened yet.

Why do women have to move furniture? I think my wife missed her calling. She could have had a great career with Mayflower or Bekins. I finally learned not to argue with her. She gave up asking me to help. Now she moves everything around while I am at work. That is why she wants me to continue working – so she can be free to re-arrange the furniture.

I must admit our Bible study did end finally on a positive note. Our leader gave us a line that has saved our marriage a thousand times: "When your patience runs out it is time to walk out." That is why I am so healthy; I enjoy walking. Whenever my patience runs out, my wife always points to the door, reminding me that it is time to walk out.

Yes, confound it, I am impatient. But I am also one lucky old man. Despite my impatience, my sweet wife has not walked out on me yet. She just keeps pointing to the door. And I get to walk a lot. +

Let your soul catch up with your body

)X(

Call it burnout. Call it exhaustion. Whatever you call it, most of us have experienced it. For me it is a time when I need to slow down and let my soul catch up with my body.

Exhaustion is no mystery. We know why it occurs. We drive ourselves to the limit as though everything depends on us. This usually makes us harder to live with, and the people around us wonder what is going on.

So it was that this week I found myself in the woods of Georgia, south of Atlanta, inviting my soul to catch up with my body. It dawned on me how much I needed this time apart when my wife insisted that I go.

In that secluded place I took the time to look at an Oak tree. It needed no help from me to make shade with its multitude of green leaves. Little birds unseen made their presence known with quiet singing that calmed my spirit.

I sat in the sunshine for awhile, moving only slightly the old rocking chair beneath me. The gentle breeze made me wonder why I spend so little time sitting quietly to allow my inner wheels to stop spinning.

The water of the small pond nearby was peaceful, disturbed only by the two swans that came ashore for lunch while I was watching. They seemed not to notice me as they nervously gulped down seed from the tall grass. They are eating too fast, I thought; they'll have indigestion. The inner voice said, "You are just like them; you eat too fast too." True. No need to argue.

I was not alone during my retreat from the fast track. Some 22 of us shared the four days. All of us were there at the invitation of our friend and Soul Doctor, Ben Campbell Johnson. Ben's expertise is Christian spirituality, a subject he taught before his retirement from Columbia Theological Seminary.

Our special guest was retired Bishop Reuben Job. The depth of his spiritual devotion was winsome and stirring. We sat on the edge of our seats eager to drink in the wisdom of his years. We were not disappointed. The pathway he has walked, and continues to walk, is not an easy road. It is the road of integrity, discipline, forgiveness, compassion, and servanthood. And it is the only road worth taking.

The framework of our days was quite monastic. That is, our days began and ended with scripture, prayer, singing, and the Eucharist. While it seemed demanding at first – to gather for worship seven times a day – it proved to be a rewarding experience.

Our day began with worship and a time of contemplative silence at 4 a.m. The day ended with worship as well, allowing us to retire for bed about 10 p.m. That made for short nights but I shrugged off thoughts of fatigue by remembering that my turkey-hunting friends handle short nights with ease. If they can do without sleep to hunt gobblers surely I can do it to hunt for more of God.

The reverently structured Divine Offices, as they are called by the Monks, help you get in touch with yourself, and with God. I have discovered, to my great surprise, that reading, chanting, praying, and singing the Psalms can allow God to energize your soul.

The group I shared these days with is a hodge-podge of people from different walks of life, laity and clergy. Most of them flew in from distant places. We represent several theological persuasions. What amazed us all is the sense of community we realized – a community of loving acceptance, compassionate affirmation, and a desire to learn from each other.

The Monks need not fear; I am not after their job of serving God by constantly living a monastic life. But I can learn from them, especially from their constant focus on God and how he wants us to live.

Doing for a week what the Monks do all the time has helped my soul catch up with my body. I realize it is not a new thing. King David described it centuries ago in the greatest of all his psalms. It is simply taking time to let the Shepherd of our souls do what he does best: "He restores my soul."

For this refreshing, undeserved restoration I am, once again, truly thankful. +

Great granddaughter moving to Kentucky

Ӿ

Annabelle is leaving town and Grandma and I are grieving to see her go. Her parents are moving to Kentucky. Since she is only three years old, Annabelle had no choice in the matter.

Great grandchildren are quite precious to us. I agree with the wise one who first said, "If I had known how wonderful grandchildren can be, I would have had them first!" We feel the same way about our great grandchildren.

We have been blessed to have Annabelle and her parents attending the same church with us. I have grown accustomed, after her stay in Sunday School, to have her run down the hall to jump into my arms just before the worship service begins. That scene became a ritual and one I treasured every Sunday. I will miss her contagious smile and joyous embrace.

Grandma and I are happy for her parents, of course. Her dad, Matthew, got a promotion and a salary raise. We can celebrate that with Matthew and Jodi even though at her age a promotion for Dad has no meaning for little Annabelle.

Annabelle's Mom is expecting another child this July – this time a son. We saw the sonogram pictures this week and were astonished as usual. Modern technology is amazing. They have known for weeks that the baby is a boy. Grandma had five sons and we had no clue about each child's sex until the moment of birth.

Knowing ahead of time is nice, I suppose, but I prefer the old method of surprise. Even with the birth of our fifth son, the doctor's words were still exciting and not monotonous: "Mr. Albritton, you have a fine new son!"

Those remain five of the most wonderful moments of my life.

For awhile our pictures of Annabelle will have to do. We will not see her very often. We plan now to see her when her brother comes along in July and again at Christmastime. Christmas for sure because it is such a great time for families to get together.

We have some great pictures of Annabelle. She is absolutely photogenic. Grandma thinks of her as almost angelic though I can recall a few times when she did not sound like an angel. But even when she is misbehaving she is still a beautiful child.

Some of our most recent pictures of Annabelle were taken when she was fishing at Uncle Mark's place in Georgia. She loved that and some of the pictures of her catching a fish are priceless. Her parents already plan to find a pond in Kentucky where Annabelle can teach her brother how to catch fish.

Annabelle's Mom has promised to bring Annabelle and her brother back one day so Grandpa can baptize them. That will be a special honor but not any greater than the honor Jodi gave me of baptizing her. While living in Montgomery Jodi accepted Christ as her Savior and gave me the privilege of baptizing her.

Her baptism was very special to me. When she and Matthew were married, I had the honor of uniting her with her husband in a lovely ceremony in Arizona. When she became a Christian, I had the honor of uniting her with her Savior, Jesus Christ, in holy baptism.

By now you understand why Grandma and I are sad to see Annabelle and her parents move to Kentucky. But we know it seems best for them, and we have learned how important it is to enjoy every hour you can spend with those you love – whenever and wherever you can.

And we are not too old to dream. Matthew may get rich and invite Grandma and me to drive up and go to the Kentucky Derby one Saturday in May. That we would love to do – especially if Annabelle goes with us. +

A significant milestone

X

High school graduation exercises are almost as American as apple pie. So the month of May often includes at least one such night for large families like ours.

This year it was grandson Joseph Daniel Albritton's turn. On a sultry Friday night Joseph strolled down the aisle of a small Baptist church, leading 13 other graduates into the choir loft. The choice of music – the "Pomp and Circumstance March" – was no surprise. No graduation these days would be complete without it.

I wondered why this music is synonymous with American graduations. Having no knowledge of the music's origin, I inquired about it with my chief consultant, Doctor Google. As most music buffs know, the march was composed by Edward Elgar around the turn of the 20th Century. At the time Elgar was England's foremost musician.

The title of the march was taken from Shakespeare's "Othello," Act III. First performed in 1901, "Pomp and Circumstance" was an immediate success; the audience's applause prompted two encores. A year later the tune was modified for the "Land of Hope and Glory" part of the "Coronation Ode" prepared for King Edward VII.

But how did the popular English music cross the Atlantic and quickly become "the graduation song" in the United States? Yale University is responsible. In 1905 the college conferred an honorary Doctorate of Music upon Elgar. To further honor him, Yale had the New Haven Symphony Orchestra and other musicians perform parts of Elgar's oratorio "The Light of Life." As the graduates marched out, the "Pomp and Circumstance" March was played, and the rest is history.

So much for the march; now back to Joseph. Now 18, Joseph has become a good student and a fine athlete. He was named the Most Valuable Offensive Player of his basketball team and recognized also for his stellar performance as the place kicker of his football team. He is the oldest child of our son Tim and his wife Karen. Joseph has two lovely sisters, Hannah and Sarah.

Joseph knows that we attended his graduation not for the excitement but because we are proud of him. Pride prompts grandparents and other family members go to these exercises while the general public stays away in droves. However, those who go are always praying the same prayer – "Lord, please don't let this thing last two hours!" We ask for mercy because we have all been to graduations that lasted two hours in a hot, bug-infested stadium.

All high school graduations seem plagued by the same problems. At least one microphone never works. The leaders get confused about what is next on the program. (This we can excuse since they do this kind of thing only once a year.) Then, as the diplomas are handed out, unseemly screaming fills the air as some family and friends flaunt pleas for dignity and enjoy sounding like rednecks for the moment. But that is graduation southern style. Most of us smile and accept it like the fleas that come with that dog.

Joseph's graduation will be remembered for one faux pas that I had never witnessed at one of these exercises before. But let me put it in context.

For some strange reason there are never enough college representatives available to present awards at the various high schools. So the person presenting scholarship awards may have to rush from one school to another on the same night. Sure enough, midway through Joseph's program, a woman went forward, put her notes down on the podium, and made a brief speech as she offered the Valedictorian his award. Then she retrieved her notes and rushed out on her way to another high school.

Moments later it was discovered that in picking up her own notes, the presenter had inadvertently also taken with her the Valedictorian's speech.

His address was next on the program. The young man, Jeffrey Alan Davis, remained in his seat while the principal asked someone to rush out into the parking lot to stop the woman from leaving.

The audience, and the Valedictorian, waited in amused silence until word came that the woman and the speech were gone "without a trace." The principal turned to the young man as though to say, "Son, the ball is in your court." To his credit, and to the applause of the audience, Jeffrey Davis stepped up to the podium. He made a valiant try to recall what he had written out to say and for the most part did it well from memory. His brief remarks won a sympathetic and enthusiastic response from his audience.

We all left wondering when the college rep discovered the dilemma she had created and if she laughed as we did about the incident.

One final note. While we were proud of our grandson, and glad to celebrate this milestone achievement in his life, we rejoiced also that our prayer was answered. The graduation lasted less than an hour. This confirmed our conclusion that the leaders and teachers at Victory Baptist School in Millbrook are not only fine people, they are also smart.

I hope we can return in two years for Hannah's graduation. And whatever mistakes may occur then, I would bet money that nobody from a local college will have a chance to drive off with the Valedictorian's speech in hand. +

X

Lately I find myself hugging other men a lot – and liking it. If that seems strange to you, relax and let me explain. It may not be as bizarre as you think.

On a recent Saturday in Auburn I helped Al Jackson with a wedding at Lakeview Baptist Church. His lovely daughter Naomi was married to my longtime friend Matt O'Rielly. I had not seen Al in several years but consider him a good friend. We greeted each other with a warm embrace – something more than a handshake.

Matt, now 26, has been like a son to me since he was 10. After his dad died suddenly, Matt came to Opelika to live. His mother Vickie wanted Matt and his brother Tim to be near their fine grandparents, Jack and Jackie Whitlock. That was a wise move. The Whitlocks are the kind of grandparents every child should have.

Matt and I hit it off from day one. As a little boy he had a heart for God. I could tell he liked me and I liked him. I assisted him with a Cub Scout project and watched him mature until he became an Eagle Scout.

He wanted to play football and the coach took a chance on him. Playing football helped Matt learn the value of discipline. That helped him grow up. Matt is a finer person for having been coached by one of the best coaches in the business – Coach Spence McCracken.

As Matt matured he began talking to me about becoming a preacher. I encouraged him to be open to the Inner Voice. I told him that only the Spirit could give him the assurance that God wanted him to pursue the ministry. He listened and conviction came.

Four years at Auburn did not dislodge his desire to preach. I told him that a fine liberal arts education would help him be better prepared to share the gospel with ordinary people. The next time I see Bill Davis I plan to hug him because he helped Matt major in philosophy. Bill helped Matt believe in himself.

Matt did become a preacher and for awhile served as pastor of three Methodist churches in Lee County. These fine Methodists embraced and encouraged Matt to hone his skills in ministry.

God provided Matt a wife and more than a wife. Naomi knows

from the example of her mother how to be a pastor's wife, companion, counselor, and friend. What a precious gift from God Naomi is to this devoted young preacher. I was so happy for Matt that I hugged him Friday night at the rehearsal and again Saturday at the wedding. I held him in my arms a long time, giving thanks to God for the special bond between us.

I saw Earl Ballard the other day and hugged him for a long time. He has been such a special friend since 1989 when we moved to Opelika. How I thank God for bringing Earl and Susan into my life.

Jim Whatley replaced both my knees three years ago. I saw Jim the other day. I hugged him and he hugged me. Jim is more than my surgeon; he is my brother in Christ. He asked about my new knees. He seemed mighty pleased to hear that they are working fine – no problems. The only problem is the 78-year-old body that my Titanium knees have to put up with.

I ran into another doctor whose friendship is precious to me. When David Scott recognized me, his eyes lit up as he smiled, called my name, and quickly embraced me. His hug simply made my day. He has a way of making me feel like somebody.

My four sons usually hug me each time they come to see me. My brother Seth embraces me when we greet each other. My Uncle Wylie Johnson hugged me at the Johnson Family reunion in June. At 91 he is the patriarch of my mother's large family.

Does this talk about hugging seem weird? Is this what happens to old people? Has senility crept up on me and taken over? My mind and my body are about worn out; is that why I like being hugged?

Whatever the reason I feel no embarrassment about it. A good hug from a friend makes me thankful for my blessings and glad to be alive. As a matter of fact, it makes me feel good right now – just thinking about it. I believe I will just thank the good Lord for the men who love me enough to hug me. Then I shall go to bed and sleep well. +

Give thanks for your father's example

Ж

Early this morning I will find a quiet place and spend a few minutes giving thanks for my father's influence on my life. Sometime after Daddy died at age 93, it dawned on me that he had impacted my life in many wonderful ways.

Many significant people have colored the way I look at life. Some touched me with lovely pastel colors, calling from me a gentleness that I long ignored and is not yet fully developed. Others, like my dad, stroked me with bold colors that birthed inside me a driving ambition to succeed.

I am quite sure that my dad never decided to exert his influence upon my life. He just did it by being the person he was. He did it by the power of his example – by the way he lived his own life.

Dad was strong physically and mentally. He worked hard all day, from sunup until sundown. There was not a lazy bone in his body. When he encountered a problem he would not quit until he found a solution. He was doggedly determined to reach his goals on any given day.

Few things could deter him once his mind was made up. If the cattle needed feed on a winter day, bad weather never slowed him down. No matter that it was storming outside, that bitter, cold wind was chapping his face; he would not rest until the work was done.

I doubt that dad ever slept eight hours any night of his life. He had a routine from which he did not waver. Bedtime was 10:30 every night. He arose at 4:30, not now and then but every morning. Even in his late eighties, when he was unable to do much at all, he got up at 4:30 to drink coffee, listen to the weather report, and read The Upper Room and his Bible.

Growing up in that environment gave me a strong work ethic. Life is made for work. Get up. Get at it. Don't waste daylight. Put your hand to the plow and go, man, go. Your work comes first. Don't let anything stop you. Keep at it until you get the job done. That attitude was engrained in me from my childhood.

Dad's honesty influenced me as strongly as his work ethic. He was a man of his word. He meant what he said and he expected the same from other people. He had no patience with liars and when he caught me in a lie, my rear end got a painful reminder of how important it is to tell the truth.

Growing up I discovered that my dad had a good reputation. I was never ashamed to be known as his son. People trusted him and that meant something to me. It gave me a sense of pride that I was his son. I never heard a man speak ill of my dad and I know now that profoundly influenced me with a desire to be an honorable man myself.

Now and then I encounter children in a family who seem not to respect their mother. They ignore her authority and talk to her as though she is stupid. Such disrespect nauseates me and my father is responsible for my attitude. He did not tolerate any disrespect of Mama when my siblings and I were growing up.

We learned that we would pay a price for "talking back to your mother." To this day I am thankful for my dad's example in this, and I deplore the way some dads allow their own children to treat their mother.

Tolerating such disrespect will surely injure a marriage and a family over time.

Dad was not perfect. He was an impatient man and often as hard as nails. But I realize now that he exerted a mighty influence upon my life. He influenced my attitudes powerfully and in many ways I am the product of his example. On Father's day I remember fondly his influence and the rare privilege of having been his son. +

Retired life a lot of fun

As I neared the age of 70 I did not imagine I would enjoy being retired. I fought it, not wanting to give up the full-time ministry that had been my life for so long.

Now that I have tried it for several years, I must admit that retired life is much more fun than I thought it would be. Actually I did go back to work full-time on the staff of Saint James United Methodist Church in Montgomery. That is what makes retired living so much fun – I can still work.

It is nice to be out of the pressure cooker that comes with being the "senior pastor" of a large church. That is not an easy job. What makes it difficult is being responsible for almost everything, including a large staff. To be effective, senior pastors have to make decisions that are not always popular and well received by fellow staff members or members of the congregation.

God blessed me with the gift of delegation and that made my job easier. Any pastor's effectiveness depends upon his ability to find gifted people he can trust. Once he does that, he needs to get out of their way and let them serve. That worked for me most of the time and I remain deeply grateful to the people who trusted me enough to serve God alongside me.

In my new job as a staff member, not the boss, I enjoy being able to leave those tough decisions to my boss – and go home smiling. That helps me to relax and trust my superiors in the same way I wanted my staff members to trust me.

Will they make mistakes? Absolutely – just like I did. Success is not being perfect in decision-making; it is learning to embrace your mistakes and benefit from them. Leaders who are unable to laugh at their own stupidity will not last long in the management of personnel.

Retired living has given me a chance to get to know my siblings, something that was not possible when I lived in other places. Fortunately, my two sisters and my brother live within a half mile of my house.

After many years of being apart, we have learned to enjoy a new relationship as adults. We go out to eat at least once a month and have fun talking about growing up together and about what we have in common now.

My brother Seth is 67 and still works at a job in the county not far from home. His wife, Pearl, is retired but still works on the farm she and Seth operate.

I left home for college when Seth was seven years old so we have enjoyed getting to know each other after all those years of being separated except for holiday reunions. I enjoy his company as a man. He is the kind of man any man would enjoy having as a friend. In many ways he reminds me of our dad whom we both admired. Seth has some of the same strong character traits that dad possessed.

Sisters Neva and Margie are both widows who have demonstrated remarkable courage to carry on beyond the deaths of their husbands. I admire them for the way they have devoted themselves to the service of others.

My wife says she is pleased to have me out of the house a good deal of the time. She thinks I am easier to live with since I went back to work. Her willingness to put up with me is one of the greatest blessings of my life.

I realize I am blessed to have the strength to continue working at age 78. I thank God for that and allowing me to discover that retired living can be more fun than I ever imagined.

Whatever is around the corner is part of the great unknown. I will not allow worry to rob me of the fun I am having now. +

𝕏

Seminaries train pastors to serve churches. Some are good at it; some are not. But no matter how good seminaries are, they will be under fire until judgment day. That is because there are "liberals" and "conservatives" in every church and they love a good fight.

Lately I have heard about several churches splitting over the issue of Calvinism. People loved the pastor – until they found out he was a Calvinist. Having no stomach for such heresy, they voted the pastor out. Be on your way, Bubba; we will have none of that nonsense in our pulpit.

If they had asked me about it, I would have encouraged them to be patient. God has a way of curing pastors of bad theology. Given some time, the pastor might have had a change of heart. Most of the folks who run preachers off have holes in their theology too. Nobody is perfect although I have known several zealous parishioners who were pretty sure they were.

Instead of firing a pastor whose theology has caused people to think, why not rejoice, search the scriptures for the truth, and give thanks to God for a pastor who can be understood. Many pastors, trying to please everybody, wind up preaching ambiguous pablum that offends nobody. I remember hearing one pastor preach about patriotism and I was not sure whether he was for it or against it.

Many Methodists have no clue what Calvinism is, so the enemy must resort to other issues to disrupt the Methodists. Years ago Methodists were familiar with Calvinism. They had bitter debates, contending that Armenianism was true and Calvinism wrong.

So what is Armenianism? It all started with a man named Jacobus Armenius. He challenged the absolutism of Calvinism, insisting that men could indeed resist God's offer of grace. Calvinists believed God's grace to be irresistible. Armenius said no, a man could refuse God's offer of grace and as a result be eternally lost.

The primary issue is over predestination; is it absolute or conditional? Calvinists say God has decreed from all eternity that some will be saved and others damned. Forget free will. If you are on God's list, you are in; if you are not on his list, there is nothing you can do about it. Armenius disagreed. He died in 1609.

Over a hundred years later John Wesley, the founder of the Methodist movement, took up the gauntlet from Armenius and embraced his theology. Christ died for all men and all men have a free will to believe in Christ and be saved or to reject him and be lost. His preaching stirred a revival fire across England as thousands chose to accept salvation by receiving Christ as Savior. Interestingly, Wesley's Methodist Magazine was first named The Armenian Magazine.

Church members do like to argue – if not over theology then over property or how the pastor should part his hair. Pastors can become exasperated; no matter what they recommend, some folks will oppose it. One of my trustees once told me, without a smile, that as long as he was on the board there would never be a unanimous vote about anything.

During a season of controversy over property in one church I served, I struggled with the stress of criticism dumped on me by some of my faithful church members. A good friend in another church rescued me with a kind letter of encouragement. He gave me the key to a winning attitude.

The key was an Arab proverb I had never heard: "The dogs bark but the caravan moves on." From the moment I read that, I had the freedom to weather the storm. I let the dogs bark but their barking no longer bothered me. I moved on with the caravan.

Most seminaries do not prepare pastors to deal with the barking dogs. Pastors have to learn that lesson the hard way. But if they learn it, then they are able to stare down the snarling dogs that can be worse than the barking kind.

Shepherds have always had to contend with dogs. Perhaps that is why God provides them with a crook so they can defend his sheep – until he comes to divide them from the goats. +

The lesson of the bamboo tree

X

Our son Matt, a pastor, used the Chinese bamboo tree to remind me of one of life's basic lessons. That lesson, in his words, is simply this: "The quality things of life are rarely developed overnight – they take time."

Our generation has pretty much ignored that lesson. The cry of modern culture is for instant gratification. Patience is not a virtue in our society. We want what we want – and we want it now.

Start a casual conversation with a stranger, say in a doctor's waiting room. A popular subject likely will be how we detest having to wait so long to see the doctor.

Many traffic lights at busy intersections drive us crazy. It irritates us to wait 30 seconds for a green light. I have even been known to say to my wife, "Did you bring any peanut butter? We could fix a sandwich before this light changes."

There was a time when we could wait a few days to receive an answer to a letter written to a friend. No more. We can hardly wait a day for a response to an email message. For some of us, the days of buying stamps and using snail mail are over. We must have an instant reply.

Cooking also must be fast. Here again we are guilty. We use the microwave oven ten times more than the oven in our stove. We hardly ever turn the oven on anymore – except occasionally to dry out the morning newspaper. A wet paper becomes a crisis. Mama cannot work the crossword puzzle if the paper is wet.

So far as men are concerned, one of the greatest inventions in history is the remote control for the television. The remote allows us to stay in our recliner and change channels without moving a muscle – except the one that works the index finger.

I have to admit I love that remote. With it I can get instant relief from the loud and insane commercials that are hated by everybody but the sponsors. I look forward to the one night a week my wife lets me use it. That's the night she goes to see a movie with the girls.

That is not really the truth. On rare occasions she will surrender the remote to me – but only after she has flipped through 682 channels trying to find some guy remodeling a patio. By then the remote is smoking. I have to let it cool down before I can use it to find a baseball game.

The checkout line at the grocery store is another example of our unwillingness to wait. Who has the time to wait in a line with three other people in it? Why can't they open more lines to accommodate me? Where is the manager anyway?

Recently as I pushed my half-filled cart of groceries into a line, I noticed a woman walk up behind me with only four items in her hands. I politely pulled my cart back and motioned to her to get ahead of me. Staring at me, with a wild look on her face, she promptly fainted.

As the paramedics worked quickly to revive her, I heard her saying repeatedly, "I can't believe it; I can't believe it; that man offered me his place in the line!"

I did not wait to see if she was alright. I rushed back into the line, just barely staying ahead of a man pushing a cart full of groceries. I have my limits to practicing compassion. My time is valuable. I had no time to wait.

Knowing how impatient we all are, I realize some of you are about ready to pull your hair out. What about the Chinese bamboo tree? So let me share the story our son told.

The Chinese plant the bamboo seed; they water and fertilize it, but the first year, nothing appears. The story is the same the second year, the third year, and the fourth year – not even a sprout comes up. Then, the fifth year they water and fertilize it – and something finally happens.

During the fifth year, in a period of about six weeks, the Chinese bamboo tree grows some 90 feet! Our son asks this penetrating question: Did the tree grow 90 feet in six weeks or did it grow 90 feet in five years?

His answer: "It grew 90 feet in five years because, had they not applied the water and fertilizer each year, there would have been no Chinese bamboo tree."

So as we struggle with this maddening demand for instant gratification that threatens to rob us of our peace and sanity, we shall be wise to learn the lesson of the Chinese bamboo tree. The best things in life are not overnight wonders. Things that matter require time, patience, and careful cultivation. +

Can I finish my Dilly Bar first?

ᚷ

One lovely spring day in 1988 a group of sky divers arranged for a dive to be photographed by a woman photographer who was also a sky diver. The woman prepared very carefully for her assignment, making sure she had all the necessary supplies for her camera.

On the day of the jump the experienced photographer jumped out of the airplane along with the other divers who were eager to do their sky-diving stunts for the camera. But there was one problem. The photographer forgot to put on her parachute and jumped to her death instead of snapping some great pictures.

Her preparation was not complete. She forgot the one thing that mattered the most. Many things are valuable, but some things are essential. Which brings me to my subject: the tough job of deciding daily what really matters in life.

News reports suggest that Kansas City Chiefs star Derrick Thomas might still be alive today had he buckled his seat beat before his tragic automobile accident. If that is true, then he neglected to do a small thing that might have saved his life. It could have happened to anyone of us.

The cynic may say, as one woman did after the Alaska Airlines jet crashed into the Pacific Ocean, "When your time is up, then you are going to die, so why worry about it." She said that to explain why she was not afraid to catch another plane that day. Logical, I suppose, but a bit too fatalistic for me.

After one man's home burned to the ground, a friend said, "I'm sorry about the fire; I understand you lost everything." "No, that's not true," the man quickly replied. "I did not lose my faith in God, so I still have the thing that mattered the most to me." His attitude was much more commendable than that of the woman who was not afraid to fly.

Tim Forneris, a computer analyst, made the news last year. Working part-time as groundskeeper for the St. Louis Cardinals, he retrieved Mark McGwire's 62nd home-run ball, and gave it to McGwire with no strings attached. He was criticized by some people because he could probably have sold the baseball later for as much as a million dollars.

Forneris responded to his critics by saying, "Life is about more than just money. It is about family, friends, and the experiences you have with them." He went on to explain, "Being the person who received the ball was a great blessing to me. And being able to return it to Mr. McGwire was a real honor and thrill. I still would not trade that experience for a million dollars."

The young man, 22, neither asked for nor received any money or memorabilia for returning the baseball to McGwire. His reward was the satisfaction of believing that he had done the honorable thing. Was Forneris a fool? Not in my book. He has discovered at a very young age what really matters.

Coach Bill McCartney finally won the college football national championship in 1990. But taking the University of Colorado to the pinnacle of his profession almost cost him his family. He felt a great emptiness because he knew that for years he had neglected his wife and family while football had been his god. Leaving football, he helped to found the men's movement known as Promise Keepers. Since then he says he has found great joy in being "sold out" to God. Simply put, he discovered what truly matters.

One day a family stopped at Dairy Queen. A 4-year-old girl tried to explain to her mom and dad that it was a special day because she had invited Jesus into her heart. Her dad, wondering how much she understood about God, said to her, "So you want to go to heaven to see Jesus, do you?"

"Yes sir," she replied, "but can I finish my Dilly Bar first?"

That story leads me to this conclusion: It is tough job to decide daily what really matters. The Dilly Bar can be a tasty treat. But sooner or later we must determine that life is about more than Dilly Bars, baseballs, and footballs. What you decide really matters really does matter. +

Death of friend a wake-up call

)(

As we make our journey from the cradle to the grave, we learn to embrace the certainty of our own death. No one is passed over. The average of death is one per person.

The recent deaths of several friends has made me more keenly aware than ever that my time is coming. The bell will toll for me and for all those I hold dear. Death is relentless. That is why we call it "the Grim Reaper."

When we are young we don't think too much about dying. We think we are going to live forever. The future is before us and we have many "miles to go before we sleep."

Even when one of our peers dies young, in an accident perhaps, we figure that will never happen to us. In later years our thoughts are different. We realize that the death of someone our own age "could have been me."

Bob Baggott's sudden passing was like that for me. I was two days older than Bob. He would have been 68 on March 26.

When we were together Bob and I joked about our age. We did not "feel" old. We still had the energy to run circles around younger men. I saw Bob everywhere, full of life and enthusiasm, serving people in a hundred different ways. I admired Bob's "get up and go." I felt that if he could do it, I could too. And he felt the same way.

Then one morning the news came. Bob was gone, "in the twinkling of an eye." And the sobering thought hit me: you could go the same way, out like a light. No more sermons to preach. No more babies to baptize. No more time to hold my wife's hand and tell her how much she means to me. No more time to hug my sons and their wives. No more time to enjoy the sweet embrace of our precious grandchildren.

There is an awesome finality about death. Life is over, done, finished. All those piles of unfinished projects will be merely a nuisance to be quickly swept aside by those who remain. No more need for the "things to do" list. Letters and cards we had hoped to respond to will go unanswered. Sentiments we had planned to express will never be known by the people we had planned to write.

Forgive me if these thoughts sound gloomy or disturbing. That is not where I want to go with all this. I do want to "stab some people awake" who may be asleep at the switch of life. The death of a good friend or loved one can be like a "wake up" call. It can prompt us to re-order our priorities and begin earnestly to put "first things first."

It can cause us to stop our busy activities long enough to ask if we are paying attention to the real purpose of living. There are key questions that need to be asked: Am I spending my days doing things that benefit other people? Am I chasing the "almighty dollar" to the neglect of those who are dearest to me? Am I collecting things or building relationships?

If life is a warehouse, then collecting things is an acceptable goal. But if life is a journey, then accumulating "stuff" is not as important as friendships. What, at the last, do we want our children and friends to say about us? Do we want to be known for our toys or our deeds of love and mercy? Do we want to be remembered for our acquisitions or our achievements, for our collections or our character?

Imagine your children standing beside your grave on the day you are buried. What would you like to hear them say? "Dad was good with his hands" or "Dad always made you feel good about yourself." "Mom never missed a day at work" or "Mom showed us how to make a house a warm and loving home."

We may choose how we shall live -- but only as long as we have breath. So if you are breathing right now, decide how you want to live this day. Make the right choices today, for none of us can be certain of tomorrow! Choices really do matter. +

The legacy of Bob Baggott

)(

At least a dozen people called me Wednesday, each wanting me to know about the death of my good friend, Bob Baggott. Like everyone else I could hardly believe the news that Bob was gone.

Whatever we mean by the phrase, "living legend," I believe it applied to Bob. He was about as well known as any man who lived in Lee County. I can still remember how surprised people were when, moving here in 1989, I had to admit that I did not know Bob Baggott. It seemed that everybody else knew him.

His reputation could be summed up in one phrase: "He's the funniest man you'll ever meet." Funnier than Lewis Grizzard? The answer was, "Well, almost, but Bob's humor is much cleaner." For a long time there was no one I wanted to get to know more than the famous Bob Baggott.

That opportunity came when Bob and Betty moved back to Opelika from Birmingham and began to serve the Farmville Baptist Church. Never one to stay in the back of the pack, Bob began running an ad in The Opelika-Auburn News. The ad included his picture and the information that his ministry was "As conservative as the Word of God, and as liberal as the Love of God."

The ad was an example of Bob's innovative style. Every time I saw the ad it made me ask, "Why didn't I think of that?" When newcomers to the area asked me about Bob, I always said, "He is the only preacher in Lee County whose picture is in the paper every week." I frankly envied his creativity.

Bob's outgoing personality won him friends everywhere he went. He was indeed "liberal" in caring for others. He had a gift for giving you a lift, making you feel worthwhile. An encourager he was in every sense of the word.

Every time I ran into him, whether at the hospital or at some community event, he went out of his way to compliment me for my ministry. Before I could brag about something he had done, he was praising me for something I had done. As I look back on it now, I realize that every time I encountered Bob he made me feel good about myself.

Bob was liberal in the use of his time and influence. Just last week he showed up at a cooperative ministry meeting for no other reason than to say by his presence, "This is a good thing you folks are attempting to do." He was there simply to encourage the efforts of his friends.

Younger preachers could benefit from Bob's example. He refused to stay bottled up in his study preparing sermons. He did not limit his ministry to the affairs of his own congregation. Wherever people were trying to help other people, like the work of the Boys and Girls Clubs or Habitat for Humanity, Bob was ready to offer a helping hand. That trait required that he find time to be involved with many community ministries.

Bob was easy to get to know. Never one for formality and titles, he enjoyed being simply "Bob." I cannot remember a single time I ever heard someone call him "Doctor Baggott," even though he had a doctor of ministry degree. He was content to be "Bob" to people in high places and low places. I admired that about him.

I had many things in common with Bob. We both loved Auburn, especially the football team. Bob was the chaplain of the football team for many years. What preacher would not have envied that honor which Bob enjoyed so much! It was but one more example of his conviction that a preacher needs to be deeply involved in his community, and always with the hope of promoting not himself but the Kingdom of God. Bob did that superbly.

We both loved humor. Sharing funny stories was Bob's forte. Never at a loss for words, Bob could have an audience in stitches within minutes. In getting to know Bob I discovered that he deserved the reputation of being "the funniest man you'll ever meet."

Funny? Yes, Lord, Bob was funny. Known for his hilarious humor, he was invited to speak everywhere. Only a few weeks ago he spoke to the seniors of our church and had them howling. My wife said, "He had me laughing so hard that tears were running down my face!"

Wednesday night at their home Betty and her family were receiving many people who, like my wife and me, were simply trying to do what Bob was always doing so well -- offering comfort and encouragement. We all had the same words on our lips: "It's so hard believe he is dead."

It is hard to believe that one who was so full of life, with so much to offer, has departed. Bob was the kind of man everyone hates to lose. What is not hard to believe is that, though dead, Bob is now more alive than ever before. He has gone home, there to add his voice to the glorious laughter of heaven.

What is easy to believe is that Wednesday morning the Lord Bob loved said to him, "Bob, it's time to come home now. I have another assignment for you. There is a group of saints up here who never learned to laugh before they got here, and I want you to tell them some of your stories."

We will miss Bob but we will never forget his legacy. He reminded us of the value of laughter in daily life. He showed us that to know God is to learn how to live, to love, and to laugh. That is a legacy that will last, for which all who knew this contagious man of God may give thanks. +

Where in the world is Zambia?

҉

Where is Zambia? That is the question many have been asking when they learn about our plan to fly over there.

Well, it is a long way from Alabama. So far in fact that it will take us about 25 hours to go from Atlanta to the airport in Lusaka, the capitol city of Zambia. Upon arrival we will "lose" more hours since Zambian time is eight hours ahead of Alabama time.

Zambia is in southern Africa. Once known as Rhodesia, the nation gained independence from the United Kingdom and took on the name Zambia in 1964.

Zambia is landlocked, having no coastline. It is surrounded by these nations: Tanzania, Angola, Malawi, Namibia, Congo, Zimbabwe, and Mozambique. Zambia is slightly larger than the state of Texas.

The country is considered "tropical" so far as its climate is concerned. We understand the temperature will range from the 60's in the daytime to the low 40's at night. July is wintertime for Zambia. We chose not to go during the rainy season, which is October to April.

You might wonder why, if the country is so large, there is so much poverty. Why not use the land to grow food for the people? The reason is that less than seven per cent of the land is fit for cultivation! That is bad news for a nation of 12 million people, one million of whom are orphan children.

Zambia does have many natural resources such as copper, zinc, lead, coal, cobalt, gold, silver, emeralds and uranium. If this is so, why not combat poverty with these resources? The answer is no doubt the same the world over – the profit from these resources does not trickle down to the common people. You know – "the rich get richer while the poor get poorer."

HIV/AIDS is a major problem in Zambia. Some 250 die from this disease every day in Zambia or nearly 100,000 annually. About 20 per cent of the adults are infected with HIV/AIDS. Because of this and other health and medical problems, the life expectancy there is 40 years. Less than three per cent of the people are 65 years of age or older. The median age is about 16.

The risk of major infectious diseases in Zambia is very high. For that reason our team has had several immunizations for protection. Since it is recommended that we not drink the water, some of our team will be drinking a lot of Cokes and all of us a lot of bottled water. We are not going there to get sick but to help people who are sick.

Another question people ask is, why go to faraway Zambia when you could help the poor in your own back yard? Some may fault us for going. After all, the money it will cost to fly could have bought a lot of food and medicine for poor people.

That is true. Still we are persuaded to go. The most obvious reason for going is to obey the command of Jesus, "Go into all the world and make disciples of all nations." So we have no choice but to go in obedience to his command.

But there is more to it than that. We have friends there who need our help. They are more than friends; they are family to us. Surely any of us is willing to make some sacrifice when a family member calls for help. It is as simple as that. They need us; we are going, by the grace of God.

None of us could go without help. Many, many people are helping make this trip possible. In a sense they are going also since we are going in their behalf. All of us feel very blessed by the support of our family and friends.

Are we concerned about hopping a plane and flying so far from home? You bet we are. But we have a vision that is bigger than our fears. By going we can build bridges of friendship and love.

We can encourage our brothers and sisters in their ministry to their own people. Our hosts, Alfred and Muumbe Kalembo, need affirmation and love just like we all do. Our being there will mean much more than the money we take them or the work we will do. And we can learn from them what it means to serve Christ in the conditions in which they choose to live.

The bottom line is that we can make a difference for children. We cannot save many children from hunger, poverty, and AIDS, but we can save a few. We can give a few children a chance for a better life and to know that Jesus loves them. That, good friends, is reason enough to get on that plane and go do what we can. +

Grandmother risks flying to Zambia

X

Today will be an awesome Sunday for our Mission Team in Zambia. We will travel over poor dirt roads to worship in the villages where our hosts, Alfred and Muumbe Kalembo, were born. With our African brothers and sisters we will praise God for all that he has done.

Missionaries made it possible for Alfred and Muumbe to receive an education. They had to walk for miles to school because there were no schools in their villages. There was no medical clinic in their villages, no fresh water, and none of the facilities we consider necessary for civilized living.

Conditions in those villages remain about the same as they were when Alfred and Muumbe were born. There is one difference –a new well now provides fresh water in each village. The people no longer have to walk to a nearby stream to bring back contaminated water for cooking and cleaning.

Each of these wells was drilled and put in place by funds given this spring by members of the Frazer Sunday School Class of Saint James United Methodist Church. The cost of installing each well was seventy-five hundred dollars.

Today we will dedicate each well to the glory of God and praise God that fresh water is now available to these village people. I know we will all tremble as we stand beside these wells and witness what love can make possible when people care.

It was not easy to decide to fly to Zambia. Some of our friends questioned the wisdom of our making such an arduous trip at our age. But we felt God calling us to do it. One of our sons said to his mother, "Do you know how much it will cost for us to bring your body back if you were to die in Africa?"

That question prompted my wife to think seriously about the trip. Perhaps, she thought, we should just send money and stay at home. Sometimes the result of Dean's heart-searching is a poem. Here is her touching response, titled "Bury Me in Africa":

Bury me in Africa if that is where I die.
My body will be useless no matter where I lie.
I will be finished with this earthly shell.
The best part of me has another place to dwell.
Don't weep that I have died on foreign soil.
It is not foreign to Christ; He died for all.
Don't mourn that you cannot stand beside my grave,
But rejoice that my heart was strong and brave.
"She had nothing to give," the critics may say.
"She should have stayed home to pray."
The words they say sound so very true
But the word from God is what I must do.
So if you should read that I died in a strange land,
Just give thanks that I followed our Lord's command:
"Go into the world and make disciples of men
And I will be with you to the end."

Dean composed this poem on February 9. She added a footnote that she had written the poem "for my African children Lumba, Chile, Chipo, Lindi, Lulu, Muumbe, and Alfred. They would keep my grave with tender loving care and place wild flowers there."

Since then she has not looked back. Her face has been focused toward serving Christ in Zambia. Despite her physical difficulties, her indomitable spirit has been an inspiration to her teammates: Bill McDurmont, Dan and Lisha Adam, Jill Davis, Brad Davis, Scott Kaak, Tim Albritton, Joseph Albritton, Steve Albritton, Robert Albritton, Edwin Baldwin, and me.

Perhaps this will explain why I consider it a privilege to tag along with this great grandmother and serve by her side. I think we all see this trip as an act of obedience. To God be the glory! +

Love and the ministry of presence

֍

The trip to Zambia and back was exhausting. Underline that. In fact, it was more exhausting than we had imagined. It takes a long time to fly halfway around the world.

Without any sleep Sunday night we boarded a Delta jet that took us to Dulles Airport in Washington. No problem. We made our way to the gate for Ethiopian Airlines where the problems began. Our flight departed three hours late so we missed our connection in Addis Ababa. An unplanned night in the capitol city of Ethiopia pushed our total time of travel to 55 hours before arriving at our destination – Lusaka, Zambia. We left home Sunday night and stepped on Zambia soil Wednesday afternoon.

Our delay turned out to be a blessing. Physically worn out by the time of our arrival in Addis Abba, we got much needed rest. That helped us get ready for a grueling schedule that began a few hours after we arrived in Lusaka. After collecting our baggage we were greeted in the loading area by an ensemble of singers who welcomed us to Zambia in song. Dressed in their colorful native shirts, they humbled us with their beautiful greeting.

We were taken straight from the airport for a worship service at the John Howard Church in Lusaka. The name of the church confirmed for me that we were destined to be in Zambia. John Howard is one of the finest Christian men serving the Lord at our home church – Saint James United Methodist Church in Montgomery.

The people – especially the children – welcomed us with open arms and warm hearts. Dozens of children were eager to shake our hands then, and every time we arrived at the church to worship with them. Their awesome praise team was on the stage as we walked in.

The music was loud, beautiful, and inspiring. We were swept away by the way they expressed their love for Jesus in song – and dance. Zambian Christians can hardly sing without swaying and dancing. Most of our team of 13 got into the rhythm with them. Home folks would have laughed to see us dancing in the aisles!

Impressed with the sight of so many children in the congregation, I preached about Jesus' love of children. Later I realized that this was the reason we were there – the love of Jesus. Truth has never been more wonderfully expressed than in the simple song that says it all – "Jesus loves the little children, red and yellow, black and white, they are precious in his sight. Jesus loves the little children of the world."

The next morning we began ministry in several arenas. Some of us began working – in Vacation Bible School fashion – with a group of children that grew to more than 350. Others began leading a conference for women and a conference for pastors and church leaders. Still others began working on improvements at the home and headquarters of our hosts – Alfred and Muumbe Kalembo who direct the work of International Leadership Institute for Southern Africa (ILISA).

Another team departed for Livingstone to participate in conferences concerning the use of land. A forester in our group met with a Zambian forester to discuss wise and creative ways to use the land provided to the Kalembos by the government.

Our team saw God at work. We did not take God there; He was already working there in ways we knew about and in ways we never dreamed. We learned so much from the people. We learned much about their land, their need, their shocking poverty, and the determination of God's People to serve Christ faithfully there.

We came home by way of another exhausting trip but this time missed no connections. We were back on American soil within 30 hours. Tired but thrilled with the positive impact of our mission to Zambia, at least on ourselves, we found welcome rest in our own beds.

I slept for 12 hours but not before thanking God for the awareness that missionary work is not about serving other people. It is all about accepting people with love and encouraging them to remain faithful to the Christ. As much as anything missions is about love and a ministry of presence. Our host, Alfred Kalembo, summed it up: "The greatest gift you have given us is your presence, just being here with us to love and encourage us." That says it all. +

Dean's reflections on Zambia

Adam was lonely so God made Eve for him. Walter was lonely and God made Dean for me. Together we have traveled to five of the world's continents. We have met wonderful people everywhere we have visited, but none more charming than the gracious people of Zambia.

Dean has a vivid imagination. She sees things other people miss. She expresses her feelings well in poetry and prose. I hope you will enjoy reading a few of her observations about our recent journey to the African nation of Zambia. Here are Dean's reflections:

Forgive me for repeating a few facts that you already know about Zambia. Yes, it is halfway around the world; it is a poor country. AIDS is a very serious disease that is killing more and more people every day. Dust and wind choke your breathing passages to the limit, but all these facts fade away when I think of some of the people who made an impact on my life while in Zambia.

Catherine is Alfred Kalembo's sister. I learned about her a few years ago when Alfred shared a little about her life with me. She is a single mom with one daughter, Linda. I didn't ask a lot of questions about why she was single, but I felt a strong desire to help her. Several times I sent her boxes of clothes and later I sent her some money through Alfred.

When our team arrived at Alfred's home on the outskirts of Lusaka, the first person who greeted me was Catherine. We both held each other for a long time. There were no words because she does not speak English. Over the nine days I was in Zambia Catherine became more precious to me. Linda is a shy seven-year-old who is receiving a good education, the kind that poverty denied her mother Catherine.

Why was my heart so touched by Catherine's plight? I discovered that she had birthed seven babies over seven years. Yes, she had a husband, but when she could not produce a child that lived, he deserted her and got a divorce.

She was left to care for herself as best she could. With no education there was little she could do. Alfred helped her open a little restaurant in Lusaka. Soon it was clear that she was in deep depression and someone had taken advantage of her. She was pregnant with Linda.

When she gave birth to Linda she needed to be with Alfred and

Catheri:

Muumbe. He and Muumbe took her into their home, where she has been since that time. She needs a home of her own and she may soon have one thanks to the Frazer Sunday School Class at Saint James. The class has sent her a little money for several months. With that money she bought a small lot and has built a concrete foundation for what will be her first home other than a village hut.

I stood on this foundation with Catherine, Alfred, and one of her friends and prayed over this land. I had a vision of this house being completed. A well was dug by hand and it furnishes water to the people around Catherine's lot. Where water gushes from the rock, I believe God is there.

Catherine held on to me for as long as she could. When it was time for us to go to the airport, she got into Alfred's car and sat beside me. She walked as far as she could with me and when I looked back she was wiping tears from her eyes and so was I. I will not forget Catherine. I plan to continue helping her until I know that she has a home.

Alfred's life began in a rural village named Siansowa. His mother, Maria, and sister, Catherine, gave up everything for Alfred to get an education. It is no wonder that he is trying to help them in every way he can. Maria does not speak English so I had someone say to her that whenever Alfred is in America I treat him like a son. Like Catherine, Maria bonded with me instantly.

She loved our son Matt when he came to her village five years ago. There were those times when Maria and I could say nothing but love each other with our eyes. There was a knowing look that was like looking into eternity. We stood side by side when the well was dedicated in the village where she and Alfred grew up. The overflowing well that we prayed would never run dry is a great blessing to this village. The well was installed with funds donated this spring by the Frazer Class.

When we got on the bus to depart, Maria got on board to hug me once again. We both knew that we would never see each other again on this side of heaven, but Maria is a survivor and I know she will be alright even in that impoverished village.

Who would ever think that you would meet a boy named Anxious? We met him at the school where he is in the 11th grade. Walter gave him a new name -- Perfect Peace. Anxious is one of the orphans being supported by the Frazer Class. AIDS robbed him of both his parents. We were delighted to see him and learn that he is very bright. He dreams of being a doctor and I have no doubt that he can achieve what wants to do. His teachers gave us a good report on him. I plan to stay in touch with this young man and encourage him in every way I can.

Hannah became my interpreter during the time I shared with the women in a three-day conference. She had such wit and wisdom. It was a great blessing to meet a lady who lives among the poorest of the poor and still continues to give her time and energy to the church. She was the pastor's aide.

She copied my poem, "I've Done my Share," for all the women and made me feel very special. On Tuesday night when we had our last service, she gave me a gift – a piece of crochet. The note read, "Whenever you look at this crochet, please remember me." That will be an easy task, for Hannah, like several others, will be in my heart as long as I live. +

Fourteen eating at a table in Zambia

)(

Four weeks in Zambia by no means qualifies me as an expert on that large nation in the southern half of Africa. But it was a beginning that left me with strong impressions of the land and its people.

Zambia is not a beautiful country. Much of what I saw was barren and rocky. Trees were scarce and much of the land is not cultivatable. Around Lusaka, the capitol city, hundreds of people spend all day in the fields chipping small pieces off of the granite embedded in the ground. They sell the chipped rock for a pittance. One woman said she made five dollars on a good day.

What is beautiful about Zambia is its people. Zambians are beautiful people. They are a peace-loving people. War has not scarred Zambia since it became an independent nation in 1964. A government official told me the country is becoming more and more stable. "In the last election," he said, "the people gave the President a mandate. He is working hard to keep his promises."

Missions comes alive when you put a face on it. So let me describe some of the faces that motivate me to care about the work in Zambia. There are the bright faces of our adopted son and daughter, Alfred and Muumbe Kalembo. Both were born in remote villages. Against all odds both obtained an education. Alfred recently completed a doctor of ministry degree conferred on him by Asbury Theological Seminary. He and Muumbe have five handsome children.

When Alfred and Muumbe (pronounced MOOM-BAY) talk about their ministry to fellow Zambians, their faces light up with a holy joy. They are optimistic to the core and determined to rescue some of the underprivileged thousands all around them. HIV-AIDS has orphaned a million children in Zambia alone. One child at a time, the Kalembos are placing orphans in Christian homes where they will receive food, clothing, and the opportunity to attend school.

On a wider scale Alfred and Muumbe are serving together as regional directors of the International Leadership Institute, a global ministry that is training Christian leaders on every continent. ILI's goal is to train ten thousand leaders around the world every year, men and women who in turn agree to recruit and train others in the basic core values of the

Christian faith. The Kalembos are doing their part by holding training conferences in Zambia and ten other nations. So far the response to their training has been incredibly positive.

When our team met with the Kalembo family recently in their home, Alfred introduced 14 people as "family" members. One was his sister Catherine who is responsible for the gardening on the land around the home. Catherine has very little education and does not understand English, though it is the official language of Zambia. But she is a diligent worker and oversees the care of vegetables needed to feed the large family.

Twenty large sacks of corn, harvested recently, are stored in the garage. Though it is now winter in Zambia, there were several rows of luscious tomatoes growing beside the house. A picture of Catherine's charming smile, as she stood beside the beautiful tomatoes, is a treasure I brought home last week. Catherine's farm work is supported by the Frazer Sunday School Class at our church.

Catherine has birthed eight children. Only one, Linda, has lived. The others were still-born. A couple in Alabama decided last year to help Linda get an education. This generous investment in Linda has paid off handsomely. She is now in the seventh grade and makes good marks. The expression on Linda's face was different from a year ago. The difference was the hope and dignity now shining in her lovely eyes. She has a chance and she knows it.

A little boy named Pasco was one of the 14 now eating at Alfred's table. No one told me where the lad came from, only that his parents died of AIDS. He had never been to school. Our team got together some money so the Kalembos could enroll Pasco in school. Soon he will have a new uniform and begin school for the first time. Embraced by the Kalembos, he also has a chance – and a family as well.

A family in Elmore County donated a water pump for the Kalembo home. One day Alfred called my attention to a water faucet in front of the house. "We put it there," he said, "so our neighbors could share our water. Some of them walk half a mile to come get water here." We took pictures of three young women who had come for water. Each smiled graciously and giggled while we marveled at their ability to balance a five-gallon container of fresh water on their heads.

In Zambia we saw water buffaloes, elephants, giraffes, deer, wild hogs, baboons, and monkeys. Each had a face that was strangely different from human faces. But what impressed me the most were the striking faces of the Zambian people – people needing help and people providing help. Those faces, some hauntingly unforgettable, linger in my mind, motivating me to do more than pray for them. Most prayers need hands and feet that God uses as he answers. +

✕

Seven years ago seven African Christians became part of our family. Our son Matt introduced us to his friends Alfred and Muumbe Kalembo and their five children. Like Matt, Alfred was in seminary seeking a degree in theology. The two became instant friends.

We invited the Kalembos to our home for the Christmas holidays and found them to be charming people. Their spirits meshed with ours. Within days we made the unanimous decision to "adopt" each other spiritually. They are like family to us, and we to them. Since then my wife and I have been Mom and Dad to our son Alfred and our daughter Muumbe. Their children are our grandchildren.

We knew almost nothing about their homeland, Zambia, a small nation in Africa. Our appreciation for it grew the more we learned from Alfred and Muumbe, and from our son's report of his visit there five years ago. The possibility of our walking on Zambian soil at our age seemed quite remote.

After Matt and Alfred finished seminary, the Kalembos returned to their home in N'Dola, Zambia, where Alfred would begin teaching young pastors in a Christian college. Soon an unusual opportunity opened up for Alfred.

He accepted the invitation and began serving on the staff of International Leadership Institute. His assignment is to train and equip native Christians in ten southern African nations including Zambia. ILI is enlisting gifted leaders across the world for the sole purpose of training Christians who can equip hundreds of other Christians in their own country with the skills of evangelization.

His new work made it necessary for Alfred to move his family to Lusaka, the capital city of Zambia. He secured a house there that needed a lot of work to make it livable. There Muumbe set up another school for small children, similar to the one she has been operating in N'Dola. In addition, the government has given Alfred 40 acres of land provided he develops it and makes it productive (within 10 years).

The bottom line is that Alfred needs some help with this new house, the new school, and the land. So his need for assistance has felt like a call to come over to Africa and help. Right now I am trying to put together a team of ten to twelve people who will pay their way to Lusaka and help this family make the transition. By doing this we can free this gifted man to spend his time and energy equipping, encouraging, and enlisting native Christians in southern Africa to teach hundreds of their fellow citizens the good news of Christianity.

By July when hopefully our team flies to Zambia, my wife and I will be well into our 75th year. As we contemplate this mission, there is an old man inside me who is waving red flags and telling me that I am foolish. This old man tells me that there are plenty of people in Alabama who need help and we are too old to fly halfway across the world.

This old man is wise and he has a rather convincing argument. Frankly I am often tempted to follow his advice. But as of this moment I have chosen to listen to someone else – the young man inside me.

The young man keeps telling me about Islamic terrorists who are willing to kill themselves to fulfill their insane mission. He tells me the world needs people who will show these terrorists that there are other people who are willing to make sacrifices for a much greater cause.

I like the way this young man inside me talks. So I have decided to fly to Zambia and do what I can to help the Kalembos fulfill their mission to reach ten nations for God.

Have you ever thought about spending two weeks in Zambia doing some work for God? Like the Marines, I am looking for a few good men – or women – who will accept the challenge. If you feel the itch, scratch it by calling me. Otherwise, just throw up an earnest prayer that our mission will succeed. +

My new Zambian brothers

X

The names of many Christians in Zambia are surprisingly different from American names. My interpreter for three sermons preached in Lusaka was a winsome and intelligent man named Never.

Out of respect for him I refrained by laughing at his name although my host and African son Alfred chuckled when he introduced Never to me. He realized it would sound funny to me and of course it did.

Since normally I would not ask a new acquaintance why his parents gave him a strange name, I did not ask Never to explain his name to me. I was left to wonder. Was his birth perhaps a surprise? Did his parents "never" expect to have a son? I have no idea.

I did resort to a play on words when we parted company. As I embraced my new friend who could translate Alabama English into Tonga, I said, "I will never forget you, Never, and I will always be thankful for your friendship." He smiled affectionately.

Last names are seldom given in introductions in Zambia, at least among Christians. I came away with no idea what Never's last name is. While we were together, he was Never and I was Walter. Titles mattered little. In fact, not a single person was ever introduced to me as "Mr." or "Mrs." That facilitated a sense of family that could be warmly embraced.

Genesis was one of our gracious hosts for the week in Zambia. A dear friend of Alfred for many years, Genesis works in the office of the president of Zambia. He is an accountant by trade and highly respected by his peers and friends.

We learned that Genesis had taken the week off from his work to assist us in our travel in the country. At several points along the highway, our chartered bus was stopped by armed police officers who inquired about the nature of our business. When Genesis, recognized as a government official, offered an explanation for our group, we were quickly given permission to proceed.

In a roadside market Genesis saw me struggling to understand what might be a reasonable price for a wood carving. He came to my rescue and told me what to offer the man badgering me to buy his wares. The man quickly agreed to accept my offer of ten dollars for a carving he had insisted was worth fifty dollars.

Well dressed, intelligent, and informed, Genesis helped our team feel welcome and secure. His presence during our entire visit proved to be a very special blessing. I never asked but I guessed he must have been his parents' firstborn child.

We met Anxious at his school along the main highway from Livingstone to Lusaka. He is an orphan, both of his parents having died with AIDS. A rising junior in high school, Anxious is 17 and a good student.

Our team chatted with him outside the school and took pictures. He is a handsome lad, serious minded, and disarmingly friendly. His support of three hundred dollars a year is being paid by the Frazer Sunday School Class in our church.

When I met Anxious that day I felt compelled to give him a new name. No one should have to live his entire life named Anxious. So I said to the young man, "Today I give you a new name. From now on your name will be Perfect Peace."

Anxious smiled, said nothing and left me guessing that he was probably thinking to himself, "This dear old man from America must have a screw missing somewhere." Still I hope one day to hear from Anxious and to see that he has signed his letter, "your friend, Peace." He wants to go to college and study medicine. I am "anxious" to help him do that.

Because of their unusual names, some of my brothers and sisters in Zambia will be easy to remember. I was told there was a man there named Carburetor and another named Generator. One of the children we met was a pretty little girl named Memory who needs help to go to school. Whatever their names, they are now members of my family for they are my brothers and sisters in Christ. +

Is the world about to end?

$\mathcal{X}$

Are we living in the last days of the world? Some people are convinced that the end of the world as we know it is just ahead. Yet predictions of the world's end are not new. Such prophecies have been made for at least two thousand years and to date they have all been wrong.

One prophetic writer advanced the idea that "666," the number of the beast mentioned in the Bible, is actually the date for the beginning of the Rapture – 06/06/06. Obviously he was wrong since that date is now history.

One man said the Rapture would begin on the 7th hour of the 7th day of the 7th month of the Hebrew calendar in the year corresponding to 2007. He was wrong. Another writer has predicted that global warming and the melting of the polar ice caps before 2012 will signal the beginning of the end.

The War of Armageddon will begin, says another prophet, at the precise moment the population of the earth reaches 6.66 billion people. Quite possibly the world population has already surpassed that number.

The predictions of Michael Drosnin caught my attention. In his book, The Bible Code II, Drosnin offered the startling conclusion that coded in the Bible are the words "atomic holocaust" and "World War" as well as the year 2006.

Drosnin might have more creditability had he not advanced the idea that the DNA of the human race was brought to the earth in a space vehicle by beings of higher intelligence who live somewhere in the universe. This also the Bible code revealed to him. That is simply too much of a stretch, at least for me.

Earlier this month Dr. Bernard Lewis, an expert on the Middle East and a professor emeritus of Princeton University, drew serious attention with his article in the Wall Street Journal. He suggested that the nation of Iran might have a cataclysmic event planned for August 22nd.

That date on the Islamic calendar is significant to Muslims who on that date celebrate the night flight of the prophet Mohammed on a winged horse to heaven and back. We breathed a sigh of relief when no nuclear attack upon Jerusalem was reported on that Tuesday.

Lewis, however, helps us understand a striking change that has occurred in recent years. Not too long ago world leaders were in agreement that the use of nuclear weapons would result in mutual annihilation. So no nation at war has been willing to use such deadly force since America used it in World War II.

That apparently is no longer true. Radical Islamic leaders, like the current president of Iran, may be willing to use nuclear warheads now because of their relatively new attitude toward life and death. Radical Muslims are now willing to kill themselves, and their own people, without remorse because they believe killing infidels pleases God. The media reports this every day as suicide bombings are accelerating.

They can embrace this unthinkable (to us) attitude because of their conviction that when they die Muslims go straight to heaven while the rest of us go straight to hell. So killing fellow Muslims is doing them a favor by sending them to heaven sooner. These Muslims have a mission – death to all infidels.

If you still have any doubt about the thinking of Islamic terrorists, consider this chilling quote attributed to Osama bin Laden:

"The Americans love life; that is their weakness. We love death and that is our strength."

This statement epitomizes the radical change of attitude toward life and death that is being embraced by a growing number of Muslims.
Despite all the predictions that the end of the world is near, and the uneasiness we all feel about a possible nuclear holocaust, we must not allow ourselves to be obsessed with fear. It still makes sense to believe that "This is my Father's World, and though the wrong seems oft so strong, God is the Ruler yet."

So far as I can tell, God has not surrendered his sovereignty over the world to ruthless terrorists. He is still in charge and will be until he decides, in his own good time, to close shop. Until then I suggest we continue to sing with confident joy, "The Lord is King; let the heavens ring! God reigns; let the earth be glad"! +

What really matters

҉

Conflict takes a toll on everyone. No one is immune to the wear and tear of stress. It does its damage, silently and insidiously, on the inside of the mind and the body. Outwardly we may manage to smile but inwardly we are churning.

Sometimes we bring trouble on ourselves. At other times it just shows up, like a sudden thunderstorm, without warning. Friction or a dispute becomes a heated skirmish and people begin taking sides.

Church and community fights are like that. A dispute can mushroom quickly into a fierce struggle. People can make accusations, express harsh feelings, and an argument can have a life of its own. Antagonists bait friends and family members, urging them to take a stand. Some will even resort to intimidation to gain strength for their side.

Some people can get so embroiled in disagreements that they become irrational. When that happens these feuds feed on emotion and calm thinking is nowhere to be found. Overnight friends become enemies over issues that do not merit the loss of friendship.

When we find ourselves in the middle of such hostility, it will help us, no matter what side we are on, to step back and take a few minutes to remind ourselves what truly matters. Stunned by an ugly disagreement in my own church, I paused to reflect on what is really important to me.

First, things are not as important as people. People matter. Things are here today and gone tomorrow. We can do without things; we can get some more stuff. But losing a friend is a devastating experience. So friends are important. They are so important that we ought not to give up on them because of a difference of opinion.

Second, truth is important. Lies lose. Rumors rot. Deceit fails. Truth on the other hand will never let us down. It is like solid rock while deception is like shifting sand. So truth matters and it pays to stand by the truth at all costs.

Third, respect is important. One of the great treasures of my life is the respect of my wife, my family, and my friends. Because respect means so much to me, I must refrain from conduct that might rob me of the respect of those who have faith in me. So even when my adversaries stoop to lying and slander, I must take the high ground rather than retaliate. Respect is so important, then, that I must resist the surge of anger and resentment that can slip so easily into my mind.

Fourth, obeying God is important. Many good causes beg for our devotion. Many people are eager to tell us what we ought to do. But we can get so caught up in trying to please people that we overlook what God wants done. Ultimately the only approval that really matters is the approval of God. We are all accountable to God. He has a plan for living and he expects us to follow it. When we fail or refuse to obey God, we lose the only thing worth saving - the chance to hear him say one day, "Well done." So obeying God is so important that often we must refuse to do what other well-meaning people want us to do so that we may please God.

Finally, love is important. Love wins. Hate loses. Stir up hate and dissension and you will live to regret it. Breeding strife is like spitting into the wind. Sooner or later you will pay for it because you will lose respect for yourself as well as the respect of others. Those who love win in the long run. Those who ignore love and insist on having their own way may win a skirmish but eventually they will lose the war.

Life is truly difficult. There are issues and conflicts that sometimes bring us to our knees. But one thing is sure: it always helps to step back and take a few minutes to remember what really matters. +

5924889R0

Made in the USA
Charleston, SC
21 August 2010